W9-BJL-888

PSYCHOANALYSIS
AND THE QUESTION OF THE TEXT

Psychoanalysis
and the Question of the Text

 Selected Papers
from the English Institute, 1976–77

New Series, no. 2

Edited, with a Preface, by Geoffrey H. Hartman

THE JOHNS HOPKINS UNIVERSITY PRESS
BALTIMORE AND LONDON

Manufactured in the United States of America

The Johns Hopkins University Press, Baltimore, Maryland 21218
The Johns Hopkins Press Ltd., London

Library of Congress Catalog Card Number 78-7656
ISBN 0-8018-2128-2

Library of Congress Cataloging in Publication data
will be found on the last printed page of this book.

Contents

Preface   vii

Critic, Define Thyself
  Murray M. Schwartz   1

How Can Dr. Johnson's Remarks on Cordelia's
Death Add to My Own Response?
  Norman H. Holland   18

The Psychology of Criticism, or
What Can Be Said
  Cary Nelson   45

The Notion of Blockage in the Literature
of the Sublime
  Neil Hertz   62

Psychoanalysis: The French Connection
  Geoffrey H. Hartman   86

Coming into One's Own
  Jacques Derrida   114

The Frame of Reference:
Poe, Lacan, Derrida
  Barbara Johnson   149

The English Institute, 1977   173

The Program   175

Registrants, 1977   177

Preface

This volume does not contain something for everyone. It reflects the considerable and, one hopes, fruitful complication of psychoanalytic studies as they accept their mutual rather than masterful relation to language and literature. Those who expect literary case studies will be disappointed. Interpretations that focus exclusively on a literary text and perform a certain number of analytic moves—mainly of the reversing kind, so that love is also shown to be hate, or a concealed motive is disclosed, or the echoing of "faeces" in "faces" is proposed—seem to be as dated as certain kinds of Gothic shudder. Every essay included here is, if anything, too conscious of the changing vocabularies and modified models of applied analysis, and particularly of the inadequacy of the applied science model of analysis itself. The emphasis has shifted from producing yet another interpretation, yet another exercise in casuistry, to understanding from within the institutional development of psychoanalysis, and from the inner development of Freud's writings, what kind of event in the history of interpretation psychoanalysis is proving to be.

Freud's work was redemptive at first, almost in a religious way. Dreams received meanings and were no longer excluded from the covenant of significance. The dumb eloquence of psychosomatic symptoms was recognized. Wit and art were the dream-work passing through the barriers of civilized speech into the daylight world. But there remained a feeling that psychoanalysis was needed only for the cure of this "extraordinary" language. It was a science "of" those language states; and the "of" was not yet felt to be ambiguous. But now the "of" has become ambiguous, and it denotes a more complicated if not complicit relation between scientific or objective modes of knowledge and their materials. As the distinction between extraordinary and ordinary language becomes less certain, the language of science is questioned. Does it really escape being figurative? Does it not have its own metaphors, or "flowers of speech"? "Pathology literally speaking is a flower garden," wrote William Carlos Williams. "The study of medicine is an inverted sort of horticulture. Over and above all this floats the philosophy of disease which is a stern dance. One of its most delightful gestures is bringing flowers to the sick."

The increasing, grating prevalence of the word "discourse" is another sign of this perception. We ask: What kind of discourse is literary criticism? What is the status of psychoanalytic discourse? Can these be honestly distinguished from the discourse they take for their text, from poetry or art or somatic writing? Or why does the work of art seem more lucid than the "ridiculous terminology" (Antonin Artaud's phrase) that claims to elucidate it? Even when these difficult questions do not aim at a hermeneutics of indeterminacy, they suggest what the psychoanalytic precept means, that we should learn to tolerate ambiguity and ambivalence.

In short, the logic of inquiry produces a text that raises a question about the text so produced. My title for the present volume reflects this problem. But it is fair to add that none of the following essays are scientific rather than literary. They are *en voyage*, passing through psychoanalysis, which seems to be passing through itself, and no destination is assured. The priority of a sensibility informed by literature means that all terms claiming to be termini are scrutinized. The term is the block. Literature destabilizes, by overdetermination or indeterminacy—by what seems to be an excess (figurality) or a defect (equivocation)—the "real character" of communication.

Yet we always deal, at some point, with given passages: a Shakespeare sonnet, Wordsworth's description of a London beggar, Dr. Johnson on *King Lear*, Freud's *Beyond the Pleasure*

Principle, Jean Genet's florid fictions, an autobiographical phantasy of Walter Benjamin's, Jacques Lacan on Poe. Often, as in Jacques Derrida, Neil Hertz, or Murray Schwartz, the "passage experience" becomes itself the focus. How does the scrupulous reader pass from word to word, or from rhythm and body feeling to meaning, or from Addison to Kant to Freud? Or how does he pass from one specialized idiom or genre, such as criticism or science of mind, to another, such as autobiography or fiction? The question that moves to the center is that of the character of the written character: its ambiguous origin and uncertain effect, its metaphorical energy however restrained or purified, its residual bodily or hieroglyphic aspect, its irreducible "sounddance" (Joyce).

Even though no essay deals at length with character in the other sense (reflections, spurred by psychoanalysis, on the development of personality and the genesis of identity), we are not trapped into pure verbalism. The chameleon poet, Keats said, thinking of himself and Shakespeare, delights as much in an Iago as an Imogen. "As to the poetical Character . . . it is not itself—it has no self—it is everything and nothing—It has no character . . . no Identity." But precisely because "it" has no identity, we find in Freud a movement toward enlarging the scope of the stabilizing "ego," which assumes in his later writings an expanded capacity to integrate the unconscious processes ascribed to the "it." Coleridge's emphasis on "the *Ego*, its metaphysical Sublimity—and intimate Synthesis with the principle of Co-adunation" (that is, with imagination as a unifying as well as empathizing faculty) goes in the same direction. As Robert Langbaum has said, in a book suggestively called *The Mysteries of Identity*, "unity is the issue," and "more than words like *self* and *ego*, *identity* emphasizes the problematical nature of the self's unity." The brief yet powerful tract by Lionel Trilling, *Sincerity and Authenticity*, should also be mentioned as raising this issue within a perspective that remains literary but assimilates in a highly critical way both Freudian and sociological currents of thought.

To restate the Keatsian paradox: lack of identity *characterizes* the poet. The New Criticism interpreted this paradox in its own way. The identity lack was associated with flexibility of spirit, with the testing of premature statements through such devices as irony, ambiguity, and the creation of dramatic personae. The writer's tolerance of "no identity" reappeared at the level of the sign or "written character" as a masterful handling of ambiguities and made them incremental forms of rhetorical mastery within an enlarged conception of poetics. Literary language was to be distinguished from nonliterary in terms of this special poetic logic. Thus the New Criticism may be viewed, in retrospect, as a parallel development to ego psychology. Just as the latter complicated the notion of soul or self, so the former complicated the notion of the unity of the artifact. What mattered to both was that the regressive or archaic or overdetermined qualities of symbolic expression should stay in the service of the ego.

Yet, as Freud remarked in *Beyond the Pleasure Principle*, "much of the ego is itself unconscious." The New Criticism, however, maintained a descriptive vocabulary stressing the conscious or manipulative side of literature. It was rhetoric indeed, but used so as to disabuse us of rhetoric and to prevent unconscious capture by psychological or ideological simplifications. Yet what does it mean for art to be in the service of an ego when "much of the ego is itself unconscious?"

Today, by many thinkers in France, and especially by the psychoanalytic movement associated with Jacques Lacan, the unconscious ego is identified with language, or the priority of language to meaning. Literary language (the "lack" or "gap" in meaning that leads to figurative supplementation or overdetermined and ambiguous usage) is not treated as specifically literary: it is said to characterize the very structure of the psyche. Whereas for Norman Holland (more explicitly even than for Empson) unstable or referentially problematic meaning becomes a positive literary feature that evokes responses that can be added up, for Neil Hertz (who works on the border between the New Critics and Continental thought) so much of language is *not* resolvable as meaning that literature becomes a way of subverting what it cannot stem: the drive toward containing language within meaning. As in a Peter Handke play, self-identity is not possible without speech, and speech is not possible without the categorical hope for meaning, yet speech continually gives the lie to the fictional alliance between identity (the ego) and meaning. Hertz also extends the problem of identity and of multiplying responses into the realm of secondary texts and invokes Kant's notion of a "mathematical sublime" to help him define the mind that faces that particular chaos.

The statement that language is not meaning relies, of course, on a disjunction between (referential) meaning and (nonreferential) signification. On this matter Anglo-American critics remain as divided as I. A. Richards was: he had a real appreciation of figurative complexities and what he called literary "pseudostatement," yet he also kept urging utopian proposals for Basic English and a scientifically efficient, or disambiguated, mode of communication. By now, at least, the concept of identity in the ethical or psychological realm has been linked to the problem of reference in the linguistic realm. Moreover, if the "character" of the poet seems opposed to "character" as a defensive or fixed identity, it is no accident that those who remain within the fold of ego psychology have been busy with Shakespeare. Could they but establish an operative concept of identity in a poet who seems to have no identity, then ego psychology might hold its own despite subversive pressures from the Continent.

I do not claim that the essays in this volume show a definitive advance over previous modes of psychoanalytic criticism. In fact, they contain literary criticism only if we expand the notion of what is literary or—since expansion sounds imperialistic—if we do not reify what is literary. The closest, most intense analysis here is Derrida's, and it bears on Freud's own text: the *fort/da* episode in the second chapter of *Beyond the Pleasure Principle*. How do we classify that book after reading Derrida? Is it psychoanalysis, philosophy, literature, or autobiography? These are not exclusive genres, of course; yet Derrida meditates on the written status of Freud's text more insistently than any literary critic. We are made aware that the institutional character of the science of psychoanalysis stands in relation to the institutional character of writing itself. Freud, that is, becomes Scripture, as the interpreter returns to a text with the strength to be foundational. Whether we revise or criticize or interpret that text is less important than the fact that we return to it.

The structure of that return also fascinates Barbara Johnson, since it involves the very possibility of a "just" criticism. But justice here is not equated with correctness. The relation of secondary to primary, of commentary to the object of commentary, is so dialectical that the "frame" of reference becomes more important than what is being referred to—Poe's story or its true interpretation. We are shown that one writer is necessarily "framed" by another, so that we remain within a crime story even when the genre seems to be critical interpretation. Derrida frames Lacan's interpretation of Poe by claiming that Lacan set false boundaries to the disseminative force of a writing whose logic is "parergonal"—whose boundaries are always crumbling. Johnson does not side with Derrida or Lacan: she stresses the inevitability of the problem of framing in this complex, intertextual situation. Instead of seeking to adjudicate divergent interpretations, she shows that the interpreter cannot find a stable place from which to observe literature (fiction or analysis) as an object, so that a relativity theory emerges that is remarkably precise. Because of Lacan and Derrida, Poe's *Purloined Letter* continues to circulate in a relay that finds no end, yet nevertheless reaches its destination insofar as there is a coincidence of sender and receiver, of writer and reader. But everything depends on how this coincidence is understood.

The Derrida essay on Freud, published here for the first time, calls for special comment. It deals with Freud's dream-children, that is, his masterful hope of being not only a father but also a founder, the absolute father of the institution of psychoanalysis. But what it remarkable is not Derrida's thesis so much as his style of reading. *Beyond the Pleasure Principle*, or that portion of it describing the famous episode of the grandchild's game with the wooden reel (it has been interpreted by many successors, including Lacan), is subjected to a reading so close as to become dreamlike. Freud's text is shown to be consumed by the very dream logic he discovered. A radicalized "literary" reflection on the persona who writes this book brings out a multiple subject (writer, father, grandfather, founder) and a multiple object (the *fort/da* game; the relation of the pleasure principle to a "beyond"; filiation; dissemination, or projecting psychoanalysis into the future yet trying to master that future by repetition). Derrida, in this way, not only overdetermines the "scene of writing," he actually inserts the writer into it. "Just as Ernst [Freud's grandchild] in recalling the object (mother, plaything or whatever), comes also to recall *himself* in an immediately supplementary operation [the *da*], in the same way the speculating grandfather, describing or recalling this or that, recalls *himself*, and produces what is called his text, making a contract with himself so as to be left holding all the strings of his line, descendants and ascendants, in an incontestable *ascendancy*" (see p. 134 of this volume).

It may surprise the reader that an analogue to Derrida's project—or rather, to what he reveals of Freud's project—is Keats's attempt, in *The Fall of Hyperion*, to enter the scene of the dream in his own person, as if he were a god among the gods, and his being searingly, punitively shown up. Before Keats there was, of course, Dante; and going still further back to those who traffic with dreams we come to the original "speculator," Joseph, who dwelt as a lord in the land often associated with the invention of hieroglyphic writing, the land of Egypt.

By making Freud's text unreadable in terms of a scientific thesis (concerning what lies "beyond" the pleasure principle), Derrida produces an *a-thesis* (his own word, rhyming with ascesis), which defies the progressive and pedagogical ambitions of psychoanalysis. Derrida's fussy parentheses ("please grant me all these parentheses"), elaborations, qualifications, repetitions, etc., serve to perplex the forward movement or "beyond" of our *libido sciendi*, and disclose instead "the blurred syntax of the genealogical scene" which is here intrinsically linked to the act of writing and to a new understanding of autobiography. After reading (unreading) Freud's text in the light of Derrida, we realize that the troubling question of the relation of person to persona, of author to text, has been exponentially deepened and can no longer be closed off by literary-critical fiat. The so-called "genetic fallacy," as well as theories of artistic impersonality from Mallarmé through T. S. Eliot, are defensive gestures that reveal the unfathomable and ghostly extension of what Freud himself termed "family romance": speculation about one's ancestry and one's progeny, and in the case of Freud a kind of science fiction, the establishment of canonical texts that would guarantee the future of an institution that is not an illusion. Yet, since no thesis can survive Derrida's parentheses, it is the force of Freud's illusion we are left with.

Ideally, psychoanalysis should provide a closer mode of close reading. Instead, it often blinds the "scientific" interpreter to the use of language, his own as well as that of the text at hand. The reductionist types of reading that result add nothing to theme, symbol, and archetype hunting. What does it matter that the drift of an interpretation is descendental rather than ascendental, that sex rather than a lofty ideal proves to be the key? Such concepts as sublimation or regression in the service of the ego or defensive mastery do not compensate for the crudeness and tactlessness of these ventures. That the patient—in this case the text—survives is something of a miracle. Today we read these older kinds of interpretation (Freud's excepted) only to know the worst. It is to get them over with, to face the vigor of certain reductionist moves, to admire the artist for the odds he overcame, or ourselves for staying relatively sane though born *inter faeces et urinas*.

Yet some of the older interpretations remain more forceful than the accommodated and scrupulous inquiries we have praised, not simply because demystifying analyses bring a cathartic and gratifying shock. They do, of course, challenge the very pretense that what we call mind has genuinely integrated infantile and instinctual determinants. The "riddle of the sphincter," as Kenneth Burke called it, may be more moving and ludicrous than Derrida's "riddle of the sfeinctor." The main achievement of the older criticism, however, is that it revives in us the sense of *hierarchy*: the tremendous effort it takes to order and subordinate, so that even if that effort (called civilization) leads to repression or to a self-disturbing rather than settled happiness, it remains as heroic as Wordsworth proclaimed:

> O heavens! how awful is the might of souls
> And what they do within themselves . . .

Wordsworth is alluding to the heroic age of childhood ("while yet / The yoke of earth is new to them, the world /Nothing but a wild field where they were sown") but we know that this age never ends. "The Child is Father of the Man."

Freud's science of mind contains a heroic argument worthy of epic poetry. It evokes episodes of divine rage, murderous

jealousy, gigantic superstition, foundation fever, self-destroy-
ings and self-creatings. Earlier psychoanalytic interpretations
were often based on the myth of the sick artist, popularized in
Edmund Wilson's *The Wound and the Bow*: suffering and
strength were said to be inextricably mixed, neurosis and art
went together. "To the artist," Trilling remarked in an essay of
thirty years ago, "the myth gives some of the ancient powers
and privileges of the idiot and the fool, half-prophetic creatures,
or of the mutilated priest." And it is true that with Freud we
reenter a world supposedly mastered or left behind: not history
so much as prehistory and biology, which irrupt again in the
form of enacted fictions, involuntary sympathies, ambivalent
phobias and symbiotic delusions. The possibility of a cure, in
this world, is precarious to the point of being Kafkaesque.
"There could be no doubt that little Hans was not only *frightened* of horses; he approached them with admiration and
interest. As soon as his anxiety began to diminsh, he identified
himself with the dreaded creature: he began to jump about like
a horse and in his turn bit his father" (*Totem and Taboo*).

That is funny and grim at once. The milder models of psychoanalysis, however, that are now gaining favor and that again
use the terms "psychology" and "psychoanalysis" interchange-
ably, already belong to an era in which Freud has become a
gruff yet kindly uncle instead of the stern father and founder he
was. It would be ironic if he were to yield nothing for literary
studies except a greater freedom of critical style and an awareness of the interplay between art, criticism, biography, and
other reified genres. I would like to think that the studies of
Murray Schwartz, Cary Nelson, and Norman Holland border on
a more daring perspective. For, though the physician cannot
cure himself, the interpreter can define himself, and he can be
asked to consider his own standards and status in the light of
the psychoanalytic precepts he is applying. The reference or aim
of his work cannot be purely outward, directed exclusively

toward the object of description: ever subtler notions of transference and countertransference, of hermeneutic complexity
when it comes to discerning what is literal and what is figurative, as well as a better knowledge of the role of "transitional
objects," put a new burden on the *interpreter's* language. The
language of interpretation realizes it must share bed and board
with the object language.

Yet to emphasize the syntonic element (or a symphonic play
of identity themes) at the expense of the hierarchic, may
denature not only the findings of Freud but also an achieved
literacy. It may represent literacy as too liberal an acquisition.
The mutilated priest disappears then into the eager-worded,
responsive student. Strong speech, mythic or figurative, is allied
to muteness, muteness to mutilation. Psychoanalysis, a mode of
dream interpretation and the decyphering of psychosomatic
states, cannot become (without grave distortion) a free speech
movement, an evangelism of the Academy whose good tidings
expel the old, repressive word in favor of the new. Therefore,
despite cultural differences and idiosyncratic obstacles, many
essays here make sense of Lacan. He is a conservative phenomenon: he insists on the heroic Freud, on the stern or terrible
father, though at a level that, strangely enough, again jettisons
biology.

Speech, for Lacan, is not a cry of (biological) need but a cry
of desire. Like the achieved literacy of artifacts, it stands
beyond the pleasure principle; it is defined, therefore, by that
"Long Way Round to Nirvana" that also characterizes, in
Freud, the workings-out of the death instinct. The Short Way
is via the sphere of narcissistic images; but the symbolic or verbal sphere is where desire conducts its endless ballet, as in the
fairy tale whose luckless hero (sometimes villain) is doomed to
enter a dance-to-the-death. Lacan calls this dance, after Heidegger, "the subjective bringing to realization of being-for-death."

The snare of words or network of symbols, Lacan insists, is so total that it shapes our destiny more than flesh-and-blood generation. It is a second birth that precedes the first. The problematic of desire is this radical mediation of the word. It is not I (the subject) who desires; it is the object-language of desire that alienates the subject from himself in the very movement of desire and brings him to the point where this desire of the other (the "of" denoting ambiguously that the desire which flows toward the other belongs to the other rather than to me; it is his desire I am expressing) drives him to wish for a cessation of all desire. Why should I speak at all if speech merely expresses the desire of someone else, if it is not "mine" but "your's" or "their's"? To live in truth is to live in that temptation toward silence, toward aphasia, yet to maintain the "imperative of the word." For the word that is given up is not given up: it must inscribe itself somewhere else, as a psychosomatic or mental symptom.

Our muteness, therefore, is comparable to "honest Iago's" at the end of *Othello*. The only honest thing in Iago is his reversion to an enigmatic silence that implies a revolt against subjectivity: being subject, that is, to the desire of another, living in or toward his desire, condemned to be, in speech and act, an incurably envious person. "Patiently," writes Lacan, "the subject withdraws his precarious will-to-live from the sheepish effusions of Eros, from verbal symbolism itself, in order to affirm it only, at the last, in an unspoken curse." That is Iago; and we also understand better the "immense relief" suffusing Sonnet 29 as described by Schwartz. "Desiring this mans art and that mans scope," the self, when released rather than blocked by the Other, "sings himns" (hymns / him-s). Hertz's essay indicates, in a related way, how the critic's as well as the poet's mode of discourse is shadowed by blockage or a nostalgia for aphasia, a seemingly negative but deceptively reassuring inclination, reinforced by ideas of sublimity.

The essays gathered here reflect the present state of psycho-analytic criticism. Though theoretical rather than practical, they are rarely programmatic, and show how thoroughly Freud has become a source text to which we turn and return. Their scrutiny of the language of institutional models compensates us for a relative lack of new interpretations. These will come, I am sure, and are not totally absent here; but theory must first conceive of itself as productive, or as a parallel text of equal workmanship, rather than as a metalanguage.

Since my own essay adds to Freudian explorations of social psychology and Lacanian extensions of semiosis a special interest in the survival of religious forms, I should like to end by stressing the adjacency of the "Question of the Text" to issues that do not usually fall into the domain of literary criticism. To see, for example, how hierarchy affects the human economy, how institutional forms are created, elaborated, and perceived, has been a captive topic of the social sciences. Freud himself was mainly interested in the household of the psyche: in the feeding-sources and attachments of the ego, its instinctual determinants, the complex network it could not rise beyond, the way it was built and structured by dependency. The relation of the ego (understood as that in the psyche which acts with relative autonomy) to biology and archeology—obscurely evidenced in a realm called the unconscious—always eluded Freud, and his science tried to define a boundary it could not cross *as* a science, only as metapsychological speculation. Now the relation of the ego to language and signification has been added to this study of the unconscious. We are still thinking and writing at the Freudian boundary.

GEOFFREY H. HARTMAN

PSYCHOANALYSIS
AND THE QUESTION OF THE TEXT

Murray M. Schwartz

Critic, Define Thyself

My topic could be no less than the possibilities for criticism today. Yet even trying to imagine the scope of such a topic makes me dizzy, sinking and weightless at the same time. We have so many possibilities and so few common perceptions of our place in the order of things. I have moments when I hear a babble of critical voices drowning the voices criticism was intended to amplify. What a situation we are in when the lead article in *PMLA* presents a critic speaking of critics as if the trajectories of their careers had displaced the ones they write about![1] Here we seem to have a domino theory without gravity: everyone leans on everyone else, but nobody falls! Or everybody is always falling, but, being in orbit, nobody hits ground!

Perhaps we must adapt, or metamorphose. Astronauts, after all, are demonstrating that life is possible without a ground, or with an artificial ground chosen at the moment in order to get (temporarily) oriented in a particular direction, for a particular purpose. There are giddy possibilities and anxieties here. The astronaut chooses up and down, re-creating both self (as perceiver) and world (as perceived) by an act of will. He is constantly becoming the center of his own universe. His body is a variable among variables, his mind a calculator of relationships. There is evidence that his feet shrink and his head swells. Ultimately, he will become a perfect sphere, or so it seems. We do not know. One thing is certain, however. The astronaut, like the critic, lives provisionally, dependently. He is free to live in a space without time, but his experience of this space depends on his spaceship and its provisions. And even the astronaut in his ascetic indulgence must face reentry to the world that is both the source and the negation of his freedom.

As critics, we are living in a time of spacy freedom. Our

1

weightlessness is the absence of anchoring authority, and this is also a source of our gravity, our searching seriousness. We have become hyperconscious of our choices in relation to our medium, our freedom to use and use up language. We do not know our internal limits as a profession and depend instead on institutional provision to delimit our numbers, if not our methods. It is a situation we can celebrate or lament, depending on our tolerance for uncertainty (and the security of our jobs).

At the risk of contributing to the state of affairs I am describing, I want to situate myself on a borderline between criticism and psychoanalysis and to offer some reflections on the process of interpretation and the role of critical acts in the ongoing institution of criticism. The psychoanalytic side of my subject is as changing as the literary. We are no longer in a position to appeal to the formulae of metapsychology without also recognizing that they, too, are provisional and inseparable from the needs and fears of their formulators and users. There are psychoanalyses today; there is no psychoanalysis. There are schools in which psychoanalytic theorists make love and war, like critics. But there are also, I believe, new perspectives on problems as old as psychoanalysis that we can adapt to our advantage.

Let me return to my title. Seen from one vantage point, it is a command that cannot be disobeyed. How can a critic, or any speaker of words, not define himself? The speech act simultaneously constitutes the speaker and the object of his speech. This is axiomatic in psychoanalysis, a place to begin. From a Freudian perspective, Kenneth Burke's definition of man as the inventor of the negative is as true as its opposite.[2] We can never actually absent ourselves from our utterances, whether bodily or verbal. The "talking cure" depends on the fact that we are always talking, literally or metaphorically. Absence in its many forms—forgetting, denying, repressing, or just being silent—is always perceived psychoanalytically as a form of presence. The psychoanalyst asks, "In what way is this person announcing himself?" This is not to say that all announcements are conscious or verbal. The "talking cure" began with bodies speaking through hysterical symptoms that could be "converted" into words. To say that we cannot but define ourselves is merely to point to the realm of symbolic action, and its potentially infinite series of substitutions.

But I have a second reason, besides indicating our conscious or unconscious presence in our acts, for beginning with the apparent paradox of self-definition. The reason is this: even though psychoanalysis is predominantly a verbal psychology, its proper scope cannot be reduced to questions of language. Given its origin in the undifferentiated matrix of the mother-child interplay, linguistic representation always keeps its relation to bodily experience, especially to the basic sensations of infancy: fullness, emptiness, release, manipulation, and so on. Freud did not have an adequate linguistic theory to develop the relation between language and the body fully, but he did see a necessary relation between "word-presentations" and "thing-presentations" (*Sachvorstellung*). In a passage I find worth contemplating in relation to the prevalent notion that texts are autonomous entities, Freud (in 1891) said:

> The object-presentation [*Sachvorstellung*] is thus seen to be one which is not closed and almost one which cannot be closed, while the word-presentation is seen to be something closed, even though capable of extension.[3]

Freud's notion of a "thing" or "object-presentation" links words to sensory associations that are visual, but also tactile and acoustic. The "thing" in a "thing-presentation" is not a discrete object, like a table or a chair. It cannot be defined only by enumerating properties. It is, rather, a complex of associations rooted in the earliest bodily sensations and evoked by the word or rhythm of speech to which those sensations have become attached in the course of development. Bodily responsiveness to the human voice seems innate, a kind of preformed capacity to dance to language. If the word in its original existence as a differentiated entity presents an absent object, this object, from the perspective of the infant's experience, is a "thing" in the sense of Freud's term. Words are encoded in the coenesthetic experience of the body and remain inseparable from the felt order of things.

Language, then, is both self-defining and open in its relation to sensation and images of the body. The word always transcends mere textuality; it has texture in our individual experiences of it, and, inevitably, ambiguity. This may be why the text or the book, like the dream in Freud's associations, so often seems a fantasized maternal object, Geoffrey Hartman's "doublebreasted book" that is "now empty and now full,"[4] or Murray Krieger's "enrapturing aesthetic object" from which his separation is acknowledged to be illusory.[5] As readers, we embody language in an absorbing fantasy of self and other in relation. The interpreter, like the poet, may yearn for a fullness of speech like Rilke's breathing poem:

> Breathing, you invisible poem!
> World-space constantly in pure
> interchange with our own being. Counterpoise,
> wherein I rhythmically happen.[6]

In this state of being, words and things become one another, not because we have regressed to infancy, but because we have found (or created) a way to mix being and representation. In the language of psychoanalysis, the word has become "egosyntonic." We experience a "fit" of self and world, a transparency of language. Resistance seems to dissolve. What we resist, in fact, is external interference. "Don't bother me, I'm reading!"

But the experience of correspondence between inner and outer realities, this perfect mediation that feels unmediated, is periodic, a consummation devoutly to be wished most of the time. And also to be feared. We use language to keep our distance from sensation as well as to maintain or reestablish a connection of words and things. In the world of Rilke's poem there is no need for reality testing because reality has already passed the test. Self-definition has become pure rhythmic process. For a person experiencing the world in this way—whether we characterize the experience as ecstatic or delusional—both psychoanalysis and criticism are superfluous procedures. The poet, so to speak, has cured himself, or is too far out for help, or at least for shared perception of the world. Usually, however, this is not the case. We commonly use language in the transitional area between transparency and opacity, between fully realized subjectivity and a fully objectified medium.

Between Rilke's invisible poem and Yeats's "rag-and-bone shop of the heart"[7] we each voice a dynamic relation between words and things, a style or identity. In D. W. Winnicott's term, language is a "transitional object."[8] It exists neither here (in the realm of my omnipotent control) nor there (in the realm of natural forces independent of my self). Even in speech as full as Rilke's, there is still speech, and as soon as we recognize its presence, we are no longer reading. (In spite of Stanley Fish, I cannot read and tell you I am reading at the same time.) The transitional nature of language makes for a slippery, ironic doubleness characteristic of all symbolism. As I see it, language can only be a self-consuming artifact if it is also a burning bush. Transitional phenomena are *real illusions*, with equal accent on each word.

It is the transitional nature of language that makes interpretation possible and, in a sense, necessary. Let me develop this idea by reference to (an admittedly idealized version of) the psychoanalytic situation as Freud described it and as a contemporary analyst might redescribe it.

By Freud's definition, the psychoanalytic situation is both a space and a relationship or series of relationships between two

people. The space is designed to encourage regression and ver-
balization simultaneously, that is, to make apparent to the analyst and, one hopes, to the patient as well the dynamic relation
between words and things in the patient's experience of his
world. The instruction to free associate is, in effect, an instruction that the patient define himself by not defining himself. He
repeats himself primarily in words, since the possibility of
other forms of repetition has been deliberately diminished by
the analytic set-up.

In the psychoanalytic situation, Freud, as interpreter, saw
himself engaged in a heroic battle against the patient's repetitions of infantile experience. The essence of the interpretive
process was to convert repetition into remembering, "reproduction in the mind."[9] In the course of this transformation or relo-
cation of experience, the patient, bound by the paradox of
"free" association to reveal the history of his subjectivity,
learns to *separate* the past from its inappropriate projection
onto the present relation with the analyst in the transference.
The end of analysis, in this model, is the reconstruction of
historical truth, the "real life"[10] that was unconsciously enacted
in the present and that the analyst relegates once more to the
past, its proper place.

Now, what interests me in Freud's discussion of the interpretive process is not only his limiting epistemology (his repeated
efforts to *divide* illusion from "historical" reality) and his heroic
quest (his effort as interpreter to "triumph" over the repressed)
but also the suggestiveness of his thinking. The transference is an
ambiguous phenomenon, and Freud did not integrate all of the
meanings he assigned to it. The transference is (1) an illness; (2) a
repetition; (3) a piece of real life, although "provisional"; and (4)
a playground. This last meaning is especially suggestive. Speaking of the "patient's compulsion to repeat," Freud said:

We render it harmless, and even make use of it, by according it the

right to assert itself within certain limits. We admit it into the transference as to a playground, in which it is allowed to let itself go in almost
complete freedom and is required to display before us all the
pathogenic impulses hidden in the depths of the patient's mind.[11]

To my mind, Freud here recognized an aspect of the analytic
situation that his devaluation of transitional phenomena pre-
vented him from developing. He requires that the patient's repetitions in the playground of the transference display "pathogenic
impulses." He uses the patient's freedom of expression to limit
that freedom by interpreting its expression as inappropriate to
the present situation. The patient can then turn repetition into
"a motive for remembering."[12] I have no desire to question
the therapeutic power of this strategy. What I want to emphasize is that Freud situates himself in the position of a spectator
at a play of repetitions displayed before him. He places himself
outside the playground. Consequently, he has almost nothing to
say about the activity of the analyst in relating to the person of
the patient. The world of his analytic setting seems populated
by activities without human agents. "The compulsion" asserts
itself. "It" displays hidden motives. Ironically, Freud disavows
his own presence as a participant in the analytic relationship
even as he seeks to reconstruct and locate the patient's unconscious presence. In remembering the other, he forgets himself.
    My point is not that Freud is wrong, but that by locating him-
self in a privileged space outside the *interplay* of dualities he
leaves himself with only either/or choices. There is *either* the illusion of transference *or* the reality of historical and material
truth. In such a location he cannot account for (or even perceive consciously) the creative aspects of the transference or of
the analyst's constructions. If the transference is an "artificial
illness,"[13] there is no doubt in Freud's mind whose illness it is.
But whose artifice is it?
    Elsewhere Freud had recognized the formative, synthetic as-

pect of delusions as well as their regressive and pathological dimension. Of Schreber he wrote: "*The delusion formation, which we take to be the pathological product, is in reality an attempt at recovery, a process of reconstruction.*"[14] And later, in *Beyond the Pleasure Principle* he would describe his grandson's play in the "*fort/da*" game as a "great cultural achievement" because in it the child succeeded in reenacting both an absent relation and his response to it, thus bridging the gap between illusion and historical truth (the truth of loss.)[15] Indeed, he would also, in "Constructions in Analysis" (1937), see an equivalence between delusions and analytic constructions, since both elaborate a lost historic truth.[16] But Freud did not resolve the ambiguities and contradictions of his own insights. The analytic setting remained a place where the patient presented a distorted version of the past and the analyst "re-pasted" it.

A contemporary redescription of the analytic setting and process would include greater emphasis on the dialogic aspect of both the patient's and the analyst's communications, the "petition" in repetition and the analyst's response to it. The analyst does not only observe a play; he also participates in it. He both hears and overhears the patient. He can only know the patient's experience by re-presenting it to and through himself. What Freud failed to articulate was that his battle with the transference was a war game with nothing less than his own reality as well as the patient's reality at stake. The artifice of transference is the mutual creation of the participants in the analytic setting. The transference is not a one-way imposition on the patient's part, but a two-way interposition involving "parts" of both patient and analyst, including, possibly, reversals of roles. Transference is what comes between two people in the playground of analysis. It is what makes their play dramatic.

The aim of this game is not to end it but to learn to play it as fully as possible under the conditions established by the available language of the participants. The analytic space is a special form of cultural space. If in some respects it provides a respite from what Wallace Stevens called "the pressure of reality,"[17] it also shares with the larger cultural theater a complex and continual interplay of temporal and atemporal modes of representation. Not everything can be represented at all times; socially shared semiotic codes cannot always articulate our private selves. In a contemporary redescription of the analytic process, analysis is "interminable" not because historical truth is always imperfectly reconstructed, but because a perfect *mimesis* of either participant's lived, bodily experience must contend with the transitional nature of his medium (or media). Between "illness" and "real life" *is* historical existence (even in our dreams), what culture makes of nature, or language of the body.

In the analytic setting, the work of interpretation is not to exchange illusion for reality but to establish a boundary between the patient's experience and the analyst's experience and to bridge it simultaneously. (It is no accident that this way of describing the process also gives us a definition of the creation of a symbol.) What is called transference derives from the analyst's perception of a *difference* between his experience of the patient and the patient's experience of him. In the dialogue, the analyst hears the patient speaking to or in the presence of someone else. From the analyst's perspective, there is, so to speak, a ghost in the room. The analyst's wording ("spelling out"!) of this experience simultaneously articulates a difference and makes a difference. The patient can then perceive a difference for the first time. Even so simple an interjection as, "I see!" implies both difference and distance. The interpretive wording bridges the gap between subjectivities by symbolizing their relationship. The past becomes present to consciousness for the first time as it becomes consciously past for the first time. The interpretive words are a real illusion; they create what is there by substitution.

A successful interpretation is an interpersonal action that simultaneously fills a gap in the patient's consciousness, differentiates previously blurred or confused intrapsychic representations, and opens an area of experience to conscious choice. It is a form of reality testing by reality creation. Both the reality tested and the reality created, however, claim no authority for their existence outside the analytic process. What authorizes the process is immanent in the process, the experience of a convergence of repetition and choice in the life of the patient, instead of either repetition without choice or choice without a sense of personal continuity (which leads to a feeling of alienation or paralysis). In a sense, interpretation leads beyond interpretation, to a dialogue between two people in the presence of one another. The analysis can terminate when this dialogue can be carried on intrapsychically (interminably) outside the analytic setting. The end of analysis is living in cultural space.

Freud's dictim, "Where it was, there shall I become," should be understood (or reunderstood) not as an incorporation of the other to the self or a submission of the self to an other, but as an endless process of triangulation in which self and other each transform themselves through the medium that joins and separates them both. In the analytic setting, this means that the analyst as well as the patient becomes more consciously free to relate to his own lived experience as he succeeds in wording the patient's experience. His repetitions and intentions play out new variations in the attempt to represent the experience of an other. This must be true because he can only know the experience of an other by having an experience of another. The ambiguity of the possessive tells the whole story. The other's experience is inseparable from one's own. Consciousness means seeing through an other as we re-present that other through ourselves.

This reciprocity of the interpretive process and its relation to consciousness is not without its unities and its systematic aspects. It is, in fact, one of the strange (uncanny?) aspects of the psychoanalytic dialogue that the more mutual it becomes, the more fully both participants can contain the complexity, ambiguity, ambivalence, destructive rage, and reparative symbolization of their language and action without foreclosing open interchange. Foreclosure of the interplay between self, other, and medium constitutes one facet of every mode of resistance in the analytic process. The unity of interpretation attempts to *continue* the quest for more inclusive utterance. In this sense, unity is always pro-visional as well as provisional. The interpreter risks enacting his own resistance in every effort to "outer" the reality of the other. The reality he "outers" may be only his own private vision fixing the freedom of the other in the form of his desire. But without this risk (*his* "petition") there can be no answering response. Every unity in the analytic process is subject to the overdetermination of the process itself.

I wish to derive from my redescription of the analytic setting and process a definition of the critic as *a reader who makes a difference by using himself to represent an other.* I see a strong analogy between the analyst's interpretations of his patient's words in the analytic setting and critical acts in—the English Institute. The critic, like the analyst, simultaneously articulates a difference and makes a difference in relation to the text he chooses, a difference that subsequent readers can then perceive through his language. And like the analyst, the critic attempts to triangulate himself, a text (understood as a dynamic interplay of words and "things"), and an other, a speaker of the text, the author of its petitions and repetitions. In other words, I, as critic, seek to represent the embodiment of an other, an author, by what Jacques Lacan calls "an Inmixing of an Otherness,"[18] thus differentiating the other through myself and myself through the other. I transform the text to realize my experience of its author.

In this analogy, however, there is nothing that corresponds simply to the role of the patient vis-à-vis the analyst. Texts cannot be "cured." Poets can rarely hear or respond to my representations of them. The author I seek is actually always a fiction I re-create through his fictions. The other, then, in the critical setting, is an author *and* the other critics, the readers of my interpretation, with whom I can share my representation of him. The difference I make only has meaning in the dialogue of readers, the institution of criticism. The collective activity of criticism can thus be seen as an interminable "authorization" of authors. And the central problem for the critic can be seen as one of making representation "presentable," that is, of communicating in a language that can be "heard" by the audience he seeks. In this respect, Hartman's "anxiety attaching to representation itself"[19] derives as much from the politics of critical groups as from the dynamics of the interpreter's personality. From a psychoanalytic perspective, there are no *merely* rhetorical problems. The rhetoric of criticism springs from the same deep sources of wish and fear as the forms of art.

At this juncture, practice seems more appropriate than prescription. Let me, then, illustrate the process I have described by offering my representation of Shakespeare's Sonnet 29:

> When in disgrace with Fortune and mens eyes,
> I all alone beweepe my out-cast state,
> And trouble deafe heaven with my bootlesse cries,
> And looke upon my selfe and curse my fate.
> Wishing me like to one more rich in hope,
> Featur'd like him, like him with friends possest,
> Desiring this mans art, and that mans skope,
> With what I most injoy contented least,
> Yet in these thoughts my selfe almost despising,
> Haplye I thinke on thee, and then my state,
> (Like to the Larke at breake of daye arising)
> From sullen earth sings himns at Heavens gate,
> For thy sweet love remembred such welth brings,
> That then I skorne to change my state with Kings.[20]

The line that attracts me again and again to this sonnet is the stunning simile that announces the transformation of the speaker's "state": "Like to the Larke at breake of daye arising." I feel immense relief in the lift of the line and a great sense of power as I imagine the bird's effortless flight. The image is one of complete harmony between the bird and its surround, a visually powerful image of integrated nature. It is as if I had been, until this moment in the poem, moving toward the edge of a precipice or the end of a runway, and suddenly I realize the sensation of strong flight definitely present. The moment that feels especially exhilarating within the line is the precise yet unspecifiable moment when the flight begins, the crossing of the threshold from stillness to motion, gravity to levity. And focusing on the threshold image takes me to the line's other threshold, the passage from night to day, and the momentary pauses before and after the phrase, "at breake of daye," that are part of the music of the line. I find myself playing this moment backward and forward, from dark to light, light to dark, for the pleasure of crossing the boundary, experiencing the "break" and moving through it. I find it fascinating to sense how the lift of the line depends on the break in breath that goes with speaking it. The break leads me forward, like the break in a bird's flight that marks its catching of a wave of air.

Along with the experience of crossing the boundary from dark to light, and in the break of breath in the line, I come to realize that the line itself interrupts the flow of the sentence in which it is embedded. The simile breaks into the poem like a dawning and seems to enact the movement of consciousness it figures in its imagery: it is a break that announces a union, a recovery of access to the psychic representation of the absent love that sustains the poet. My sense of power comes from feeling a convergence of rhythm and sight: I hear and see the transformation of the speaker's state. What I experience is a paradoxical reversal, a separation from separation. The bird carries poet, poem, and this reader across the boundary from separation anxiety to a sense of dramatic, self-confident presence.

Along with my sense of separation overcome by a "break" in the flow of consciousness goes the poet's recovery of music in his ascent from earth to "Heavens gate," another threshold. "Bootlesse cries" become "himns": the movement is from "disgrace" to the edge of grace. This movement hinges on the earlier and opposite movement to a threshold, the movement *toward* total self-despising. "Almost" in line 9 seems important here. I feel the poet engaged in a risky courting of psychic disaster that yields to its opposite just in time, both "happily" and "haply," by a chance thought that may not be under conscious control. But once this thought occurs, "then," the movement outward into clarity and freedom of expression through the simile of the lark is linked to a feeling of inner contact with the memory of a nurturant relationship that overflows my sense of risk. Indeed, risk becomes "skorne to change," confident defiance of "Kings." Through "sweet love remembered" the poet remembers himself and regains his voice. (In fact, there is a momentary absence of the poet's "I" in line 13. Who is remembering then? But he is actively present again in the final line.)

All this recovery seems almost provoked by the intensity of pain that leads to it through the first eight lines of the poem. I feel a surplus of defect, an overabundance of unfulfilled desire. He is in "disgrace with Fortune *and* mens eyes," not only "alone," but "all alone." He troubles "*deafe* heaven" with "*bootlesse* cries," actions that seem *knowingly* hopeless. In the five-times repeated "and" I hear the poet insisting on the multiplication and amplification of his shame, frustration, exclusion, and yearning. I have a sense of desperate, frantic activity, a search in the *outer* world for some person or action that will enable the poet to master the contempt of others *and* his self-contempt, for not only do "mens eyes" look at him, but he looks upon himself as well. But even as I imagine the excruciating sense of self-exposure this search must involve, I find myself admiring the energy and will of the quest. He weeps, troubles, looks, curses, wishes, desires. What strength of need flows into such strength of action? What ironic trust in the value of the self leads to such a powerful demand to be heard and such an insistent seeking for others to emulate? I have the sense of a man compelled to enact his discontent, driven to approach the border of madness in order to find in himself the image of an other that can supply his desire for transformative expression. When he does find that image, his surplus of defect is transformed, as if magically, into its opposite, a surplus of self that overflows into dramatic assertion.

But the poet's union-through-memory with the image of a nurturant other (a repetition, I think, of the achievement psychoanalysts call "object constancy," the ability to maintain intrapsychic continuity by internalizing the absent mother), contributes to a *recurrent* pattern. The self-recovery I feel in the flight of the lark leads me dialectically back to the very situation with which the poet began. That is, his "skorne" repeats the scorn of others that defined his disgrace and exclusion. But now the roles are reversed; he states the state he suffered. Along with the poet's therapeutic remembering, then, I imagine his identifying with the aggressors he says precipitated his initial state. If he undoes separation in one sense, he redoes it in another. How Shakespearean this seems, this endless recycling of conflict through its opposite!

I could continue. I hear, for example, a recurrent emphasis on the poet's lack in relation to *men* in his world, a rivalrous dimension that may also determine my pleasure in his bird rising. Were I to pursue this theme, I would certainly find no lack of corroborative evidence elsewhere in Shakespeare's art. Further, I could go on to link this interpersonal theme (rivalry-lack-"castration" identification with the aggressor) to the political idea of property, via the play on "state," and to the religious idea of expulsion from heaven. All of these dimensions of the poem seem to me variations on the basic configuration of separation enacted and reversed through which I unify my experience of the poem.

I can only represent the poem through this unification. (Even a claim of disunity would comprise the attempt at comprehension I am calling unification.) And if I reflect on my own representation, I recognize both Shakespeare and aspects of myself. I have both derived and imposed my reading as a consequence of centering the poem on the image of the lark. The experience of the other is inseparable from my own. If I look back to the beginning of this essay I can find the patterns I found in the poem: I have circled from astronauts to interpreters to larks. But unlike Shakespeare's lark, which has a heaven to approach, I return to the institution of criticism, and what difference both my definition of the critic and my illustration make now depends on you.

NOTES

1. Cary Nelson, "Reading Criticism," *PMLA* 91 (October 1976): 801-15.

2. Kenneth Burke, "Definition of Man," *Language as Symbolic Action* (Berkeley and Los Angeles: University of California Press, 1966), pp. 3-24.

3. The quote is from Freud's monograph *On Aphasia*, a section of which is reproduced in *The Standard Edition of the Complete Psychological Works of Sigmund Freud*, ed. and trans. James Strachey et al., 24 vols. (London, 1953-1966), 14: 209-15.

4. Geoffrey Hartman, "The Interpreter: A Self-Analysis," *The Fate of Reading* (Chicago: University of Chicago Press, 1975), p. 19.

5. Murray Krieger, *Theory of Criticism* (Baltimore and London: The Johns Hopkins University Press, 1976), p. 17.

6. Rainer Maria Rilke, *Sonnets to Orpheus*, trans. M. D. Herter (New York: W. W. Norton and Company, Inc., 1942), p. 71, pt. 2, no. 1.

7. William Butler Yeats, 'The Circus Animals' Desertion," in *The Collected Poems of W. B. Yeats* (New York: The Macmillan Company, 1956), pp. 335-36.

8. D. W. Winnicott, *Playing and Reality* (New York: Basic Books, Inc., 1971), pp. 1-25.

9. Sigmund Freud, "Recollection, Repetition and Working Through," in *Complete Psychological Works*, 12: 153. In my discussion of Freud, all the words in quotes

are his. I footnote only those phrases that seem especially important.

10. Ibid., 12: 154.

11. Ibid.

12. Ibid.

13. Ibid.

14. Ibid., 12: 71.

15. Ibid., 18: 15.

16. Ibid., 12: 266-67.

17. Wallace Stevens, "The Nobel Rider and the Sound of Words," in *The Necessary Angel* (London: Faber and Faber, 1951), p. 20.

18. Jacques Lacan, "Of Structure as an Inmixing of an Otherness Prerequisite to Any Subject Whatever," in *The Structuralist Controversy*, ed. Richard Macksey and Eugenio Donato (Baltimore and London: The Johns Hopkins University Press, 1970), pp. 185-200.

19. Geoffrey Hartman, "War in Heaven: A Review of Harold Bloom's 'The Anxiety of Influence: A Theory of Poetry,'" in *The Fate of Reading* (Chicago: University of Chicago Press, 1975), p. 52. For Hartman's ideas on the problem of "presentability," see also the essay on "I. A. Richards and the Dream of Communication," pp. 20-40, especially pp. 34-36.

20. I am using the 1609 text reproduced in *A Casebook on Shakespeare's Sonnets*, ed. Gerald Willen and Victor B. Reed (New York: Thomas Y. Crowell Company, 1964), p. 31.

Norman N. Holland

How Can Dr. Johnson's
Remarks on Cordelia's Death
Add to My Own Response?

The most useful problem faced by today's literary critics is, I believe, What can we do with conflicting readings? "Useful," because one answer to that question opens up a way of reading as promising as the once New Criticism was. Call it "transactive criticism" or "poem opening" or simply "combining responses," it offers a way divergent readings can enrich one another rather than cancel one another out.

In the heyday of New Criticism, we all knew what to do with conflicting readings: Check a given interpretation against "the text," throw it out if it rests on "misreading," and keep it if it does not. Critics were to combine correct readings and reject incorrect ones until they cumulated knowledge about a given text in the manner of a science. Two challenges have arisen against this protoscientific world, however. From a great variety of starting points critics have begun to ask how texts correct or limit their own interpretations, if they do so at all. Interpretations may stem more from personal or communal constructions, myths, or ways of reading than from the text. One needs to consider the whole transaction in which the reader re-creates the literary experience rather than a text supposed to be isolated or "objective."

Moreover, we have found that one cannot combine interpretations so easily. A glance at a *Variorium Shakespeare* or *Milton* or the articles listed in *The Explicator*'s bibliography on any well-read writer (or urn) will show that readings vary too much to be summed up in any simple way. All too often, inconsistent interpretations draw on equally strong evidence, leaving no clear basis for rejecting one or combining two.

Besides, I believe I have shown that any one person has a characteristic way of interpreting poems and stories and also, therefore, a characteristic way of reading—and accepting or rejecting—other interpretations.[1] We each "transact" literature according to our different personalities. Each interpretation is singular because it is a function of the interpreter's unique identity (and of a great many other things, too: literary training, experience, culture, or social values as they are characteristically applied by the individual). Furthermore, each summing up of interpretations into a critical consensus is singular because this action is also a function of the interpreter's identity. All readings, even of other critics, are "idiosyncratic," that is, personally styled minglings of text and self.

Yet, obviously, there are regularities in reading as well as singularities. Everybody agrees that Moby Dick is a white whale. Virtually all Shakespeareans prefer *Hamlet* to *Titus Adronicus*. Almost all readers of Gothic fiction are women. The overwhelming majority of critics today (but not from 1681 to 1838) prefer Shakespeare's *Lear* to Nahum Tate's. How can we reconcile these regularities in reading with the singularity of individual interpretations? One of the most telling objections to a "transactive" model of literary experience is that it will account for the singularity of the reading transaction well enough, but not for these regularities.

To meet that objection, I shall take as my text one of the most singular—and "regular"—of readings, Dr. Johnson's expression of judgment and horror at the death of Cordelia:

> The injury done by Edmund to the simplicity of the action is abundantly recompensed by . . . this important moral, that villany is never at a stop, that crimes lead to crimes, and at last terminate in ruin.
> But though this moral be incidentally enforced, Shakespeare has suffered the virtue of Cordelia to perish in a just cause, contrary to the natural ideas of justice, to the hope of the reader, and, what is yet more

strange, to the faith of chronicles. Yet this conduct is justified by the Spectator, who blames Tate for giving Cordelia success and happiness in his alteration, and declares, that, in his opinion, "the tragedy has lost half its beauty." Dennis has remarked, whether justly or not, that, to secure the favourable reception of *Cato*, "the town was poisoned with much false and abominable criticism," and that endeavours had been used to discredit and decry poetical justice. A play in which the wicked prosper, and the virtuous miscarry, may doubtless be good, because it is a just representation of the common events of human life: but since all reasonable beings naturally love justice, I cannot easily be persuaded, that the observation of justice makes a play worse; or, that if other excellencies are equal, the audience will not always rise better pleased from the final triumph of persecuted virtue.

In the present case the publick has decided. Cordelia, from the time of Tate, has always retired with victory and felicity. And, if my sensations could add any thing to the general suffrage, I might relate, that I was many years ago so shocked by Cordelia's death, that I know not whether I ever endured to read again the last scenes of the play till I undertook to revise them as an editor.

There is another controversy among the criticks concerning this play. It is disputed whether the predominant image in Lear's disordered mind be the loss of his kingdom or the cruelty of his daughters. Mr. Murphy, a very judicious critick, has evinced by induction of particular passages, that the cruelty of his daughters is the primary source of his distress, and that the loss of royalty affects him only as a secondary and subordinate evil; he observes with great justness, that Lear would move our compassion but little, did we not rather consider the injured father than the degraded king.[2]

Johnson instances the two basic facts about the literary transaction. First, *King Lear* (be it Tate's or Shakespeare's) remains the same. Second, responses to the play differ completely. Johnson, for example, mentions those of Tate, John Dennis, and the Spectator—all different—and I suppose there is not a person today who agrees with Johnson's own preference for Tate's ending over Shakespeare's.[3]

These two facts lead me to ask several questions. First, how can we relate the invariable text to the variable responses?

Second, how can we relate those infinitely variable responses so that one person can use another's? How can we "add" them? Third, given the singularity of responses, how can one explain regularities in evaluating and interpreting particular literary works?

By using contemporary, "third-phase" psychoanalytic psychology,[4] I think I can come some way toward answering the first question. I can account for varying responses to an unvarying text by a concept of identity. Identity I define, following Heinz Lichtenstein, as a way of comprehending the mixture of sameness and difference that is a human life. I can understand sameness in a person by seeing it persist through change. Conversly, I understand change by seeing it against what has not changed. One way of conceptualizing that dialectic between sameness and difference—there may be others, but this I have found the most effective—is to think of identity as a theme with variations. Then I can adapt other ideas of Lichtenstein's and use the term "identity theme" for the continuing core of personality that I see a person bringing to every new experience. It is the grammatical and actual "I" that I perceive as the subject of all the changes. Whether or not that theme is "in" the person in some ultimate sense, it is an idea or even an intuition I *can* use to relate to that other person as a being in whose continuity I can trust. I need assume no more than that. It is the theme by which I *can* understand and feel individual actions are variations embodying both sameness and difference in a life that makes some intellectual and emotional sense.[5]

Reading literature is one of those variations. Again, using identity themes to study actual readers, I have become convinced that there is a general lawfulness in the reading process. We bring to a text certain expectations, typically a pattern of related wishes and fears, and we need to find in the text some match for those expectations. We need to make the text at least somewhat the kind of world we live toward. For the same reason we defend against the text: that is, we shape and change it until, to the degree we need that certainty, it is the kind of setting in which we can gratify our wishes and defeat our fears. As it is defensively shaped, we become able to enjoy the text, because the defense enables us to invest the events, people, and words of the text with our fantasies. These fantasies in turn, as thinking beings, we transform into some coherent, significant experience, perhaps no more than understanding the ending as an ending, but thus we confirm the transaction as a whole. Even so, one should not take terms like "defense" as fixed structures. They flow easily into one another, interacting with all the variety of organic life. One should treat them as questions as much as laws. What does this reader expect? How does she defend? What fantasies does she imbue the text with? What meanings does she make and how?[6]

Defense, expectation, fantasy, transformation—DEFT—they draw first meanings from the clinical experience of psychoanalysis, but they have larger, richer senses as well. Our expectations place the literary work in time, in the sequence of our wishes and fears, while our transformation of the work toward significance attaches it to themes that transcend the immediate concerns of the moment. Defenses define what we will let into ourselves from without. Fantasies are what we project from within onto the outer world. We transact literature along two of the great axes of human experience, the line of time and the boundary between self and other.

Further, the literary transaction, understood in this psychoanalytic way, has the same shape as other acts of perception, particularly linguistic perception, as revealed by modern psycholinguistics and cognitive psychology. That is, we perceive through a preexisting schema. What we perceive is our own self-generated schema plus the differences between that schema and what comes in from outer reality. Piaget uses the two terms *assimilation* and *accommodation*. In assimilation, we match external reality to an internal schema. We sense the contrast between the two. Accommodation is the much slower, less drastic modification of the internal schema to deal more effectively with reality. Finally, to come full circle, we could say that Piaget's and similar theories are to the fleeting acts of perception or understanding as identity theory is to all the actions of a human life.[7]

Now this is all very abstract. Dr. Johnson's reading of the ending of *King Lear* makes it concrete. From the point of view of this theory of reading, to understand what he wrote, we should begin, not with the text, but with its critic's transaction of the tragedy as a function of his identity.

Most people who have written on Johnson's personality see in him a balance of two forces. Julien Green arrives at this duality in describing Johnson's conversational style: first, his conversation covers everything; second, he talks about everything in a monologue of irrevocable judgments.[8] Similarly, Bertrand Bronson speaks of "the opposition of . . . two forces, the conservatism of intellectual attitude and the ebullient temperament." His Johnson alternately attacks authority and submits to it.[9] Walter Jackson Bate remarks the "twofold demand" on his prose. It must always reach out to collect experience, yet act as "a controlling and ordering of a restless and energetic activity." This reaching out can be seen in Johnson's love of travel, his prowls through London, and his almost pathological need for companionship with a continual flow of conversation and repartee. The need for experience, Bate notes, is one of the reasons Johnson gives for his massive learning: "To judge rightly of the present, we must oppose it to the past; for all judgment is comparative."[10]

The combination, then, of ebullience with control fuels Johnson's dislike of the merely bookish and the purely intellectual, particularly in the form of clever paradoxes that do not arrive at "the stability of truth." Yet, as Paul Fussell notes, "Johnson was always hospitable to inconsistencies so long as they constituted an honest registration of empirical actuality."[11] In the same vein, E. Verbeek, a Belgian professor of psychiatry, phrases this basic tension in Johnson as "between reality and imagination," and cites a letter to Mrs. Thrale: "The use of traveling is to regulate imagination by reality, and instead of *thinking* how things may be, to *see* them as they are" (italics mine).[12]

To me, this sense of a reality controlling imagination corresponds to Johnson's own theory of his and others' minds in which one has to ward off the dangers of imagination run wild by clinging to real activities in the real world. As a psychoanalytic critic, I would expect Johnson's childhood to provide a body model for this image of reality, both inner and outer, as polarized. I place in this context the late James Clifford's suggestion that, from earliest infancy, Johnson struggled to offset the disfiguring reality of his body by the superiority of his intellect.[13] Yet how often must the child have wished it were the other way round. How painfully he must have felt that tension between imagination and reality and how difficult it must have been for him to accept the primacy of reality. Johnson's realism, in being the fierce first article of his creed, testifies not only to the strength of his determination, but also, I think, to an underlying wish—and fear—that it might have been the other way, that the hard facts might have yielded to imagination and wish.

Deviously we come round to Johnson's fear of madness or, more precisely, his fear that his mind would be invaded by fantasies he could not control. If he polarized his world into authorities and subjects who obey or rebel, then he was likely to represent himself to others sometimes as an authority and sometimes as a subject. At times he would be a subject submitting or rebelliously attacking (like Bronson's well-known

"Johnson Agonistes"); at other times he became the authority whom others would submit to or attack. Thus, Johnson greeted even mild disagreement with a ferocity that rent the conversational fabric. More profoundly, the uncontrolled thought that came unbidden and unwelcome to his mind must have seemed far more invasive to Johnson than to someone differently constituted.

We can arrive, then, at a possible meaning for that much-vexed padlock. By obtaining, in his own word, *l'esclavage* from Mrs. Thrale, he was able to act out the shifting roles of ruler and subject in his life. In one role, he played the great social and cultural authority to whose judgment Mrs. Thrale in various ways deferred. In the other role, the six-foot literary giant submitted to the restraint and discipline of the 4'11" Mrs. Thrale, even kissing her foot as a subject might kneel to a king.[14]

In his opinions as in his life, Johnson alternated the role of loyal subject, to his God and his king, for example, with the role of Johnson himself as the lawgiver. In his own authority he would work out the same mingling of generous love and powerful cruelty he perceived in the authority of others. He was eager to right the wrongs of slaves, felons, beggars, prostitutes, and French prisoners of war, Admiral Byng or Doctor Dodd, yet in that very role of generous judge, he could object to abolishing the cruel public procession of the condemned from Newgate to Tyburn.

In his prose style no less than in his opinions, Johnson showed the same alternation. Bate calls it "the union of vigor and order": "With vigorous finality, one element is given its due, appearing permanently stabilized; and then its counterpart receives the same justice and permanence." Bate goes on to "the way in which the centripetal pull back to secure tamped-down finality can join with the outward centrifugal thrust—reaching out, expanding, or qualifying, and then reincorporating."[15]

It is Bate, I believe, who comes closest to making these observations on Johnson's style in prose and poetry into an identity theme, a statement of the unity one would find in Johnson's personality if one looked empathically at his choices through his eyes for a centering theme analogous to the central themes we find when we look for the unity in a literary work. "The need for certitude and control through order and pattern," says Bate in his first book on Johnson, "is more than matched by the exhausting compulsion to be awake to every detail, and the fear lest something relevant is being disregarded or self-deceptively given a false importance." In this view, Johnson's identity theme would involve his response to these two conflicting needs. In briefer terms, Bate speaks of "a compelling need for order and finality" that "is always being matched and invigorated, in fact uses and capitalizes on a dynamic experience and empirical openness."[16]

In his deeper, more recent biography of Johnson, Bate speaks of Johnson's "assimilative nature" as his way of digesting experience. A major defense was "the habit of leaping ahead in imagination into the future and forestalling disappointment and hurt by anticipating . . . and assimilating all that could produce them." This lack of basic trust (in Erik Erikson's sense) provided a foothold for the gnawing religious doubts that assailed this religious man and for the disabling depressions he suffered at every stage of his life. As a reaction against that loss of trust (traceable to the diseases and the mothering of his infancy) was his "powerful sense of self-demand, a feeling of complete personal responsibility." These two traits acted dialectically: "His lifelong compulsion to get all possible evils anticipated in advance, shrewdly, realistically, and digested into habitual response in order not to lose his ability as a 'free agent' and become the helpless victim of chance, caprice, or malignity," and so fail his self-demands. Thus, one finds in Johnson's prose a "powerful back-and-forth movement, where a thing is immediately given its due, stabilized with permanence of phrase, and then qualified with another position given equal justice."

Yet despite the magisterial writing, this perilous balance of assimilated danger and "merciless self-demand" could edge into excess: on the one hand, depression as a response to too much danger incorporated and now felt as within; on the other hand, "a morbid growth in the impulse to *correct* oneself and to keep on 'correcting' till the act of correction becomes an end in itself," as in Johnson's tics, "rollings," or counting compulsions. This correction could become "inevitable self-division and a savage turning of aggression against himself"—depression again. Bounded by this double threat of depression came the great creative achievement, the success of these reciprocal adaptations, assimilation and control: disappointment bravely digested into resolute, powerful writing; a self triumphantly demanded of.[17]

If we can empathize with and understand Johnson's life and works as creative variations on some such polarity as this, then we can answer the first question I asked: How can we relate the invariable *King Lear* (either Shakespeare's or Tate's) to Johnson's unique and individual remarks on the ending? His reading must reveal one particular variation on his more general theme, some particular balancing of his centrifugal assimilation of details with his centripetal need to stabilize and control those details.

Johnson states the problem of Cordelia's death by reaching out for competing claims: the balance of Shakespeare's authority against justice, hope, and faith. "Shakespeare has suffered . . . Cordelia to perish . . . contrary to the natural ideas of justice, to the hope of the reader, and . . . to the faith of chronicles." Johnson's first move in solving the problem is to introduce an authority: "Yet this conduct is justified by the Spectator." Then he balances the Spectator(s) by Dennis, who suggests a faintly discreditable motive for their position against poetical justice, namely, an attempt to defend Joseph Addison's *Cato*. Dennis offsets the Spectator but adds nothing of his own, and Johnson returns to the original problem.

This citation of authorities, incidentally, is only one of the ways in which Johnson behaves like a judge writing an opinion to explain a decision. I find it striking that the word "justice" or variants such as "justly" or "justified" occur eight times in this one paragraph—and not simply because Johnson is discussing a problem of injustice. On the contrary, three occurrences seem quite gratuitous: "this conduct is justified by the Spectator"; "Dennis has remarked, whether justly or not"; "it is a just representation of . . . common events." And in the next paragraph, where he is not discussing poetic justice at all, he speaks of the "judicious critic," Arthur Murphy, and the "great justness" of his observation.

In this context, I think it important that Johnson bases his final conclusion politically, on "the general suffrage" as the basis for his judicial analogy: "In the present case the publick has decided." I feel Johnson is contrasting "the general *suffrage*" to the idiosyncrasy by which "Shakespeare has *suffered* the virtue of Cordelia to perish."

As I read him, then, Johnson admits competing claims in order to arrive at a just and final decision between them. What is just is what brings humankind together into such large groupings as "all reasonable beings," "the audience," "the publick," "the general suffrage." Those groups will find their centrality in such final and embracing phrases as "love justice," "excellencies," "better pleased," "final triumph," "virtue," and "victory and felicity." In contrast to these ordered blessings, the single voice, even if it be Johnson's own, must mute itself: "If my sensations could add anything . . . I might relate. . . ." Johnson makes the consensual authority of justice very much outside, above, and larger than the particular self.

Note, too, how Johnson talks about sources, about other

critics, audience reaction, or his own reaction, but not about the text itself. Not for him is that "induction of particular passages" by the judicious Murphy. Rather, he explores beyond the text of Shakespeare's play, although that is, as he himself acknowledges, his first concern as an editor. Instead, he reaches out, centrifugally, to all those who would be heard on the subject of the play, the Spectator, Dennis, or the public, so as to give them an order and finality.

Further, Johnson images the play itself, not in performance, but after the curtain has gone down. I am responding to phrases like: "the audience will . . . always rise," or "the publick has decided," or "Cordelia . . . has . . . retired with victory and felicity." I feel I am hearing Johnson's strong need for closure and completeness as well as his unwillingness to be confined within the play, so to speak, his desire to reach beyond it, as with his citation of extratextual materials.

As I read him, however, Johnson's taking the role of a judge on the bench seems the most important thread in his reading of *Lear.* Listening to the competing claims of the Spectator, John Dennis, Arthur Murphy, and the general suffrage, he responds to those various voices with his other need, for an order and finality that will itself express the permanence of the shared realities of life. Thus Paul Fussell remarks how, in writing about Shakespeare, Johnson turns away from critical hypotheses by "going instinctively to the empirical behavior of actual people witnessing actual plays."[18] So here, in evaluating the death of Cordelia, he makes the evidence of critics and his own abstract reasoning about poetic justice yield to the plain blunt fact: "The publick has decided." He casts the audience in the role of jury, and even his editorial or judicial authority must be subsumed under that flat and final verdict.

In short, we can answer our first question. I can understand how Johnson's reading of the end of *King Lear* was a function of his identity (as I read it), his characteristic reaching out for an experience in order to bring it back within an ordering finality.

The second question is much more complicated, especially because it bears on the "I" in my answer to the first. How can we combine responses like Johnson's if we recognize that they are highly individual acts? Can we get beyond simply saying that Johnson was "wrong" in his verdict on the ending of *King Lear*, that is, using some other reading to cancel out his? Can I claim for my interpretation of Johnson's identity and verdict a validity that is binding on other readers of Johnson? Can we coordinate readings one to another in some more meaningful way than just listing them in sequence in a *Variorum*?

One way of getting beyond mere listing is to take Dr. Johnson's view as both an expression of and a contribution to his culture, or, as Stanley Fish puts it, his "interpretive community."[19] We might say Dr. Johnson's rejection of the death of Cordelia on the grounds of poetic justice was a typically eighteenth-century, neoclassic thing to do. It is possible to assume that there is a kind of eighteenth-century *Zeitgeist*, some great cultural tide on which the single critic makes his particular ripple (or, if it is someone as bulky as Dr. Johnson, his considerable splash).

Behind this idea is a still more fundamental assumption, I think, that there is an unchanging core of interpretation of Cordelia (established by the text) that then is modified to become the responses of various periods, eighteenth century, romantic, or modern, or of various individuals, such as this or that critic. Such a model follows from the premise that you can add or subtract the role of interpretive and other communities from a given response. I think the real state of affairs is both more complicated and more simple.

Consider the judicial form of Johnson's response. It was Paul Fussell, I believe, who first pointed out the intimate connection of the law with eighteenth-century writing, Johnson's in partic-ular.[20] Yet would it be correct to say the pervasiveness of legalism in the eighteenth century "caused" or "shaped" Johnson's response? Surely not. Frank Barber could have read Blackstone's *Commentaries* to Johnson at breakfast every morn-ing of his life and accomplished no more than spoiling his digestion. Johnson *chose* to interest himself in the law, he chose to associate with lawyers, he chose to write the Law Lectures, and he chose to write of Cordelia in the manner of a judicial opinion. It is not as though while doing parliamentary reports he caught some dreaded *bacillus barristerensis* that ever after infected his style. Rather, Johnson found the Anglo-Saxon judicial process a natural metaphor in which to assess Cordelia's death, because it reconciles competing claims through a central authority in the interests of the common weal. Differing points of view are called to the bar—thus fulfilling Johnson's need to gather in experience—and they are settled once and for all into generality and permanence through *stare decisis*, the fundamen-tal common law principle that precedents are to be followed. The pattern of competing claimants before a judge who would turn empirical facts into enduring law fitted Johnson's identity precisely, and he used it constantly.

In other words, he—and we—engage in a feedback. We relate to cultural entities like the law or *King Lear* by matching from them our expectations and our defensive strategies for achieving our expectations, by investing them with our fantasies, and by transforming cultural entity and fantasies together into signifi-cance. Yet the text rewards some of these matchings, invest-ments, and transformations more than others. We are involved with a feedback or, in less electronic language, a dialogue. My defenses, expectations, fantasies, and transformations are ways of asking questions of the text in the language of my identity. They are also ways I bring my training, previous literary experi-ence, in general, my community and culture, to bear—again through my identity. Then I hear (in the same identity language) the text's answers to the questions I ask, those answers affect my further questions, and thus I create and sustain a feedback or dialogue with the text.

Johnson's reading of the end of *King Lear* remains a unique transaction expressing his identity, but by recognizing the dialogic nature of the relationship between the man and the text, we now have two ways of looking at that transaction. As with any feedback, dialogue, or mutuality of transference and countertransference, I can stand off from the transaction and look at it from either one of the two possible points of view, provided I consider the *whole* transaction. If I am primarily interested in Johnson, I can ask, What does Johnson do with Tate's *Lear*? How does his response constitute a new variation on his continuing identity as I imagine it? If I am more interested in the two *King Lear*s, I can equally well ask, What does Tate's *Lear* do for Johnson? How does Tate's *Lear* answer in Johnsonian terms the characteristic defenses, expectations, fantasies, and transformations Johnson brings to bear, in a way that Shakespeare's *Lear* does not? The question for criticism becomes, How does that answering tell me about what the two *Lear*s do for me? For other people?

The first question looks for regularities in Johnson's literary response. The second, however, seeks regularities more general, such as the public's preference, during a century and a half, for Tate's version over Shakespeare's. There are also irregularities: the dispute between Dennis and the Spectator or the much bigger historical change in which the next century would come to regard both Tate's *Lear* and Johnson's preference for it as amusing examples of a neoclassic rage for order.

In this vein, consider again Johnson's relation to *King Lear*. For example, his shock. I find it instructive in comparison with the other two Shakespearean occasions for Johnson's fear. First, as a boy reading *Hamlet* in the basement, he was so moved by the ghost scene that he ran upstairs to see real people about him again. Evidently, the tragedy frightened him because he found it unreal and phantasmagoric. Second, his comment on the killing in *Othello*: "I am glad that I have ended my revisal of this dreadful scene. It is not to be endured."[21] Again, the tragedy presents Johnson with the element of unreality, Othello's delusion, but added to it, the smothering of a young woman. The ending of *King Lear* also presents the strangling of a young woman caused by delusion: Albany's poor memory ("Great thing of us forgot!"), which fails to prevent the murder, and Lear's madness. We shall probably never know what special meaning, if any, the smothering or strangling of a young woman might have for Johnson. Whatever it was, we do know that the presence of insanity, deception, or mistake would intensify the shock and pain he felt at Shakespeare's ending, but not Tate's. For Johnson, these chimeras would be frighteningly outside the norm of human society and reason.

Second, Johnson finds the finality so important to him more in Tate's play than in Shakespeare's. In giving his verdict on the two endings, he reaches out beyond the end of the play to moments in the theater when the public gives its verdict or when Cordelia has retired. In his edition Johnson glossed Kent's agonized questions, "Is this the promis'd end?" and Edgar's "Or image of that horror?" simply: "These two exclamations . . . are very obscure." For this pious man, Shakespeare's play offered no Christian ease, a fact we can balance against modern Christian readings of *Lear* or performances in which, at Lear's "Look there, look there!," Lear and the other actors look up from Cordelia's mouth to the skies as though her soul were flying heavenward on wires, like Little Eva's in the old *Uncle Tom's Cabin* melodramas. Tate's version offers that kind of finality, but Shakespeare's leaves Johnson reaching for a finality beyond the finality he can find in the text.

Finally, Johnson went outside the tragedy for the facts on

which to base his judgment: he talked about previous critics and critical controversies, about sources, about abstract literary theory, but most of all about the response of the audience. Johnson found Shakespeare's text, I presume, not inclusive enough to satisfy his strong need to bring human experience under a centering authority. Shocked by a non-Christian supernature, he sought to quiet it by rational, social, mutual consent.

Now, what are the questions Johnson's response leads me to ask? First, do I feel shock as Johnson does? Not really. At a moral level, I want to blame the victims rather than pity them. My universe demonstrates an unjudicious Murphy's law: If things can go wrong, they will. In such a world, one must be careful, and blunders like Lear's or Cordelia's produce disastrous consequences. I blame Lear for being foolish and fond enough to set up the unreal love-contest of the opening scene. I blame Cordelia for not being flexible enough to humor the old man and counterbalance his folly with worldly sense. I blame her, too, for not being forceful enough to settle the whole problem on the battlefield. The final scene offers me the painful and superfluous spectacle of people suffering the effects of such incapability and incompetence, and, as I say that, I realize that in my relation to the play, I am substituting individual effort for the hope of justicers above.

Johnson seeks a finality in *Lear* and does not find it in Shakespeare's version. Do I seek finality? In a way. I seek a finality of thematic interpretation, however, rather than a closure in the events of the plot. I seek a finality through my own efforts. I do not really expect justice from the world, and I think the characters who do are a little naive. I do, however, expect to be able to make sense of events in my own intellectual terms. While Johnson wants an immediate and human justice, I can settle for a theme of justice, tolerating injustice for the sake of poetry.

In doing so, I realize that I have an entirely different relation to the play from those who take an optimistic, trusting view of the universe. I find myself coming round to an absurdist view of the tragedy. That is, Lear tries in the opening scene to create a world around him that will be a "kind nursery." The tragedy teaches him not only the folly of the wish but the harsh metaphysical truth that one cannot expect kindness from "this tough world." The universal indifference of the last scene (as I read it) confirms the personal splittings of the first, and from this point of view, *Lear* becomes one of the most hopeless of Shakespeare's plays, far darker than *Macbeth* or *Othello*.

Johnson evidently did not find the tragedy inclusive enough. I, too, have a strong need to include everything in my response, particularly every textual detail, yet I find *Lear* quite big enough, almost too big. Johnson, however, satisfied his need to include experience by taking as the decisive fact about the play the audience's reaction to it. (In a way, he is being more the transactive critic than I.) I satisfy my need for inclusiveness by reading the play for image and motif, leading to all-embracing themes. I read this tragedy as a cosmological poem. Johnson wants a human reality.

My kind of inclusiveness parallels Charles Lamb's feeling that the tragedy could not be staged and A. C. Bradley's view that the tragedy could not be sustained on the human level and must be taken as cosmic poetic drama, a view taken to its limit in the readings of G. Wilson Knight, which I find deeply congenial. Johnson, like them and like me, catches onto that same problem, the relation of the play as play to the physical and metaphysical experience it depicts.

By looking at these different ways we all transact the play, I discover in a new way that *King Lear*, great as it is, fails to reconcile in these various critics' readings one of the great human polarities, between experience in the mind and experience in the physical world, the transitional space of symbolic

realities like plays. From this point of view, Lear's meaning-
less love-contest in the opening scene is an attempt to create a
safe, motherly universe; so are his vain hopes in the last scene.
Yet he fails, the other characters fail, we all, perhaps, fail.
Most important, I feel the play fails precisely as a play, as a
reality that should bridge the tension between the physical
and the metaphysical and does not.[22] And that is its triumph.

I do not mean simply that something is missing from the
play and that its absence causes a certain kind of response.
(That would be a clumsy way of reasoning: an absence causing
a presence.) I do mean that when I, Johnson, Tate, Dennis,
Bradley, or Knight read Lear—all in our different ways—we
attempt to create a relationship between the human and the
more-than-human. We all seem to feel that the tragedy does
not create a relationship that we need. By needing as Lear
needs, we can become terrifyingly aware of our own peremptory and blundering demands. We can feel in that terror, tragedy.

Taken this way, the history of Lear criticism ceases to be a
chronicling of opinions. It becomes a dynamic of individual
relations to the play, in which different people try to close
an imagined gap in the tragedy between the immanent and the
transcendent in different ways: by rewriting it, by Christian-
izing it, by turning it from a tragedy into a cosmic poem, by
reading it for image and theme rather than event and character. From this point of view, Johnson's preference for Tate's
version is no aberration; it stands in the main line of Lear
criticism (if it is possible to talk that way).

Similarly, when I ask this tragedy to establish a relation between the personal and the cosmic, I do not hear an answer;
I hear only an echo of my question, and I find this suddenly
the darkest of the dark tragedies. I deepened my response, not
simply by looking at "the text" nor by consulting just my
own feelings. I discovered something new about my relation

to *Lear* by looking at Johnson's and taking from his, questions about my own.

Using Johnson's "wrong" reading to question my own is what I mean by going beyond one reader's reading. One way I can combine divergent readings is by posing them as questions to the text or to one's own response and seeing what answers I get. I may achieve new approaches to the text. I may win new insight into our own responses or ourselves. In any case, what I will have done is to combine divergent responses, not cancel some and narrow others. In place of the quick pleasure of establishing my own superiority by judging others' readings valid or invalid, I have found a way of making any reading the occasion for permanently enlarging my literary experience. The answer I would give to the second question, How can we coordinate discordant responses?, is: establish a deeper, questioning relation to all responses—especially one's own.

We come, then, to the third and most vexing question: If each transaction of *King Lear* is unique, why do so many people account this tragedy a masterpiece? How did all their singularities become a regularity?[23]

Critics since Aristotle have sought something "in" the text to explain such regularities, but no one has really agreed on what that something is. A transactive model of response turns the question around. To say that *King Lear* "has pleased many and pleased long" (in Johnson's defining phrase), means that a great many people with a great many different identities have found *King Lear* a powerful tragic experience. That means: a great many people were able, through *King Lear*, to match their defenses and expectations and to transform their fantasies into significant experiences in satisfying ways.

Similarities do not become regularities, however, just because the text or the *Zeitgeist* remains the same. Think of the great variation in this small sampling of neoclassic readings of *King*

Lear. Similar readings occur when different readers pass similar mental strategies through the same text. Some expectations and transformations (or even fantasies and defenses) may be widely shared among audiences of a given culture and period or critics of a given "interpretive community." Nevertheless, these strategies will be applied in each person's characteristic style, mingled inextricably with highly individual defenses, fantasies, transformations, and expectations. Each transaction remains as unique as Johnson's or Dennis's.[24]

The question of literary longevity or success, then, remains: What possibilities for response did *King Lear* hold out, that all these different people could turn into satisfying actualities? In principle, at least, the transactive model of literary response provides a way of finding out why Shakespeare's *King Lear* has stood the test of time (two hundred years, compared to the century and a half when Tate's version occupied the stage). Just as I asked what Johnson found and did not find in this tragedy, I should now ask that same question about each of the responses of those millions of people who have enjoyed Shakespeare's *King Lear*: What possibilities of response did your transaction of this tragedy through your identity turn into actuality for *you*? Obviously an impossible task.

A detailed explanation of the convergence of literary responses is possible in principle, but it can come only *after* thousands have actually responded, when it may well be impossible in practice. The problem is that not even the most astute psychologist of audience response can predict human behavior in any substantial detail. One can, through the usual techniques of opinion sampling, arrive at moderately successful explanations of liking and disliking, remembering this or forgetting that, or other very general reactions. But one can no more predict one person's precise transaction of a literary text from the text than one can predict the ending of *Edwin Drood* from an interpretation of its beginning. The obstacle involved is the same: trying to infer details of action or language from a theme that is an abstraction from such details. Given the details, one can infer a theme inductively. Given only a theme, however, one cannot deduce details from it. If I knew only that *King Lear* dealt with the tension between fact and value, I could not infer any part of the text. If I were certain that Johnson would respond to *King Lear* as a problem of justice, I could nevertheless infer nothing about his particular remarks or even the general line of his decision or opinion.

In effect, I am saying that we can discover the dynamics by which individual readings become a widely shared opinion on the tragedy's value and meaning only by combining readings in a more subtle way than a headcount. One must extend the traditional theme and variations method of literary interpretation (literary or philosophical "hermeneutics," the social scientist's "holistic" or "case" method) from texts to transactions of texts. Then a transactive model of the literary response does provide an answer to the question of literary success, but not a predictive one and therefore probably not a practical one.

Even if we cannot examine millions of responses in the light of the different responders' identity themes, we might be able to examine a hundred or so. We would have to remember, of course, that we could consider a hundred responders to *Lear* a sample of all responders only if we had some reason to believe that their identities somehow typified the others'. Since each identity is in principle unique, a sample may be in principle no sample. Perhaps, however, one can see regularities in the vast range of identities. If so, that would be an important discovery about human beings as well as about literature.

Whether or not identities can be sampled, however, examining in depth many transactions of a masterpiece like *Lear* (or even a best seller) remains an intriguing task. The project would search out a stratum of knowledge about being literary and being human hitherto read only at the surface. Perhaps some industrious theorist and a generous foundation will combine to take the deeper plunge.

In the meantime, the old model, in which the text somehow "causes" or "limits" or "controls" response, has to give way to a new—the dynamic of one reader's reading—because the old model will not account for the wide divergence in readers' readings, especially if the readers are critics as gifted as Johnson or Bradley or Knight. As a metaphor, the "power" of the text has become outmoded and confusing.

Instead of a mechanistic notion of "impact," we need to recognize many possible relationships literents establish with literature: self to text, self to author, self to a character, self to an image or episode, self to a critic, self to many critics, self to culture, self as critic, self as critic to other critics (as in this essay), and on and on. In effect, we enter these different relationships thinking different aims and constraints appropriate for each of them. In one we may try to look only at the letter of the text. In another we may take the text as representing a reality external to itself. In a third we can think of a tragedy as a lyric. In a fourth we are concerned with the effect we ourselves are having. Yet we cannot simply subtract out "culture" or add in "text," for all these relationships involve a whole identity, and through identity all such entities as "text," "culture," "skill," or "audience."

Nevertheless, we are not facing a chaos of "subjectivity" or an infinite regression in which I am one reader reading one reader reading one reader reading. . . . Although I am surely that, all those readings answer to two basic principles. First, there is the matching of expectations and defenses so as to invest the text with fantasies to be transformed into significance—DEFT. This is essentially a modern statement of Freud's discovery about the literary transaction, that we respond consciously to a process of meaning we unconsciously give to the text.

Second, there is the circling between text and reader that I have been describing in Dr. Johnson's reading: the way the text answers the expectations, defenses, fantasies, and transformations he brings to it.

These two modes make up a model based in identity theory of the way literents transact literature. We can use it to ask—and answer—three questions fundamental to literary theory. First, we can understand how an invariable text occasions divergent responses as different responders transact it in their characteristic styles, or, to use the precise term, identities.

Second, although these individual transactions are unique, as different as apples and oranges, we nevertheless can combine different responses to a given text, by adding them in ourselves. I can relate to anyone else's response, no matter how much I might disagree with it propositionally, by trying it out, passing it through the text or through some other response (my own, for example), listening for answers to the questions I characteristically ask of texts and responses. We can read the responses of others so as to form new relations to a text or new understandings of our own established transactions.

Third, we can understand how responses, although unique, can nevertheless represent variations on a regularity I can articulate as different literents bring shared modes of expectation, defense, fantasy, or transformation to the text. Other regularities will involve modes of interpretation or response, leading to critical schools or "interpretive communities." Some shared strategies lead to the success of a literary work. A temporary favorite evidences itself as many literents from a given time and culture all find possibilities in it for satisfying transactions. A masterpiece is manifest in satisfactions for many different periods and societies. Although patterns of response may be shared, however, each person still applies them within an individual identity. One can, therefore, explain regularities of evaluation or method after they have happened, although one cannot, in principle, predict them before.

All these inquiries involve "passing through" or "trying on" alternative readings. Thereby one avoids standing outside of experiences, merely making curt judgments of valid or invalid. One avoids using the diversity of readings to subtract and thin out the possibilities of response. Instead, the very diversity becomes the way we can draw empathically on the great and not-so-great critics of the past and present, even when their conclusions seem as "idiosyncratic" or "ex-centric" or simply wrong as Dr. Johnson's on the death of Cordelia.

NOTES

1. Norman N. Holland, *5 Readers Reading* (New Haven and London: Yale University Press, 1975), pp. 208-16, 220.

2. *Johnson on Shakespeare*, ed. Arthur Sherbo, *The Yale Edition of the Works of Samuel Johnson* (New Haven and London: Yale university Press, 1968), 8: 703-5.

3. I was wrong. During the question period following this paper, I confidently asked anyone who shared Johnson's preference to raise a hand. As I expected, no one did. After the question period, however, one gentleman stealthily and somewhat shamefacedly 'confessed to me that he did in fact like Tate's ending as much as and maybe a little bit more than Shakespeare's. His scholarly specialty is Restoration adaptations of Elizabethan-Jacobean plays. Does that explain his preference? Or does his personality explain *both* vocational *and* authorial choice?

4. By "third-phase," I mean a psychoanalysis that has gone beyond the polarities of conscious-unconscious and ego-nonego to a psychology of self and other. See my "Literary Interpretation and Three Phases of Psychoanalysis," *Critical Inquiry* 3 (1976): 221-33.

5. Heinz Lichtenstein, "Identity and Sexuality: A Study of Their Interrelationship in Man," *Journal of the American Psychoanalytic Association* 9 (1961): 179-260. See also my *5 Readers Reading*.

6. See Holland, *5 Readers Reading*, pp. 123-28, 130-200 passim, 201-3, 209-12, 285-86. See also my "Transactive Criticism: Re-Creation through Identity," *Criticism* 18 (1976): 334-52.

7. See my forthcoming "What Can a Concept of Identity Add to Psycholinguistics?," *Psychiatry and the Humanities* 3 (1978). See also my forthcoming "Identity: An Interrogation at the Border of Psychology," *Language and Style*.

8. Julien Green, "Samuel Johnson," *Suite Anglaise* (Paris: Plon, 1972), p. 16.

9. Bertrand H. Bronson, *Johnson Agonistes and Other Essays* (Berkeley and Los Angeles: University of California Press, 1965), pp. 2, 8.

10. Walter Jackson Bate, *The Achievement of Samuel Johnson* (New York: Oxford University Press, 1955), p. 174. Walter Jackson Bate, *Prefaces to Criticism* (Garden City, N.Y.: Doubleday, 1959), p. 83.

11. Paul Fussell, *Samuel Johnson and the Life of Writing* (New York: Harcourt, Brace, Jovanovich, 1971), p. 42.

12. E. Verbeek, *The Measure and the Choice: A Pathographic Essay on Samuel Johnson* (Ghent: E. Story-Scientia, 1971), p. 156.

13. James L. Clifford, *Young Sam Johnson* (New York: McGraw-Hill, 1955), pp. 24-25.

14. It does not, of course, follow that Mrs. Thrale's regime was perverse or even pathological. Those would be brutal adjectives for what the two profoundly decent people who defined that relationship treated with care and respect.

Indeed, one psychoanalytic interpreter has made what is, to me, a most persuasive argument that Mrs. Thrale's combination of *douceur* and *autorité* (as Johnson described it in his French letter to her at Streatham) was deeply curative (George Irwin, *Samuel Johnson: A Personality in Conflict* [Auckland: Auckland University Press and Oxford University Press, 1971], pp. 49-51, 99, 105, 126-36, et passim). Irwin argues (convincingly, to this psychoanalytic critic) that Johnson's depressive panics stemmed from an intolerable mixture of love for his mother with resentment of her scolding (and, I would add, the physical disabilities he probably held her responsible for). Then, with his wife, with Hill Boothby, with Mrs. Thrale, and with the whole long succession of worshiped and worshiping women (and, I would add, his especially judgmental Deity), Johnson re-created the mother who scolded, judged, and confined him. With Mrs. Thrale, however, he created more—a transference like that a modern sufferer could establish with a therapist, within which he could confide in her and achieve, almost in the manner of a psychoanalysis, a partial cure of his depressive panics.

Charles Norman, *Mr. Oddity* (Drexel Hill, Penn.: Bell, 1951), pp. 204-8, also connects Mrs. Thrale's confining Johnson to his mother's restraints in childhood. I would point out that he wrote the famous French letter to Mrs. Thrale as *her* mother was dying. W. Jackson Bate examines the episode closely and concludes that Johnson was trying to get from Mrs. Thrale "something that would help him to get out of himself, and free him from the immense capacity for self-punishment that could so exhaust him." He also points out that Mrs. Thrale "in size and general appearance was not unlike his mother." He notes that Johnson, "the half-child part" of him, competed for maternal attention from Mrs. Thrale. (W. Jackson Bate, *Samuel Johnson* [New York: Harcourt, Brace, Jovanovich, 1977], pp. 388, 415, 438.)

Less precise, and therefore to me less persuasive, are the views that Johnson's chains embodied a struggle against unruly sexual desires (Clifford, *Young Sam Johnson*, pp. 314-16) or "trouble . . . of a masochistic nature" as suggested by John Wain ("The Padlock," *Samuel Johnson* [New York: Viking, 1974], pp. 286-92), tacitly basing his view on Katharine C. Balderston, "Johnson's Vile Melancholy," in *The Age of Johnson: Essays Presented to Chauncey Brewster Tinker*, ed. F. W. Hilles (New Haven: Yale University Press, 1949), pp. 3-14. Nevertheless, I can accept these views as supplementary to the transferential idea.

Johnson's padlock, as might be expected, has occasioned a great many psychiatric studies. They are summarized by William Kenney, "Dr. Johnson and the Psychiatrists,"

American Imago 17 (1960): 75-82, and by Verbeek, *Measure and Choice*, pp. 107-9 (although from his specialized point of view).

15. Bate, *Achievement of Samuel Johnson*, pp. 172, 171-2, 174.

16. Ibid., pp. 159-60, 176.

17. Walter Jackson Bate, *Samuel Johnson* (1977), pp. 297, 373, 8, 374, 207, 579, 381, and 373.

18. Fussell, *Life of Writing*, p. 105.

19. Stanley Fish, "Interpreting the *Variorum*," *Critical Inquiry* 2, (1976): 465-85.

20. Fussell, *Life of Writing*, pp. 42-50.

21. Clifford, *Young Sam Johnson*, p. 63. Fussell, *Life of Writing*, p. 223.

22. In articulating my feelings, I am being helped by Murray M. Schwartz's "Shakespeare through Contemporary Psychoanalysis," *Hebrew University Studies in Literature* 5 (1977): 182-98.

23. Or almost all. Let us not forget the gentleman who liked Tate's *Lear* about as much as Shakespeare's.

24. See, for example, the widely varying responses of eleven students and faculty in my "Transactive Teaching: Cordelia's Death," *College English* 39 (1977): 276-85.

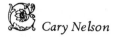 *Cary Nelson*

The Psychology of Criticism, or What Can Be Said

The first thing to be said about this topic—the psychology of criticism—is that many people believe criticism *has* no psychology. As an essentially disinterested activity, they would argue, criticism is not significantly influenced either by the psychology of the critic or by the dynamics of critical writing. So one barrier to this discussion is the collective response that its topic is no topic at all. An opposed barrier derives from another collective reaction: that the topic is essentially unspeakable and its revelations are to be avoided.

An anecdote will illustrate my point. At a conference on literature and psychology in 1977, I suggested that psychoanalysis might profitably direct itself toward an analysis of complex critical prose. One of the participants countered by saying he would be offended by any attempt to psychoanalyze his scholarship. Several people quickly pointed out the obvious irony in his position: he was quite committed to psychoanalysis as a method for interpreting fiction and poetry but was unwilling to permit its application to criticism, and especially to his own criticism. This defensive outrage can serve to characterize the second collective reaction to my topic. Both reactions are so conventional as to be exemplary. They represent, in miniature, a potential for more elaborate ways of avoiding the issues I will introduce here. If one thinks of more extended versions of these reactions—not only those reactions in print and those encountered in conversations with colleagues but also those implicit in the ideologies of scholars who have not confronted the issues openly—then one can see that discussion of the psychology of criticism is fronted by two kinds of discourse: the nonsensical and the forbidden. In much practice, of course, these are not

45

really varieties of discourse but varieties of silence, since relatively few people give voice to either position.

I want not so much to reject either of these positions as to use them, to let them reflect one another in a way that may assist the discussion to take place between them. Both positions reflect a reluctance, indeed a refusal that is collectively sanctioned, to consider the psychological dimensions of a particular human activity—the writing of criticism. This reluctance is at the core of a more general resistance to thinking about the nature of the critical activity. Imagine for a moment the potential answers to the question "What is Literature?" Few of us would be unwilling to address the subject, however unsatisfactory we might find our own answers. The complementary question "What is Criticism?" would receive quite different responses: a few disingenuously minimalist definitions, defensively moralistic platitudes, and silence. These are not only three alternate ways to react; they are also a predictable sequence or closed cycle of stances. As one fails, the critic can have recourse to the next.

I suspect that such limited responses would be sufficiently widespread that we might reasonably describe the writing of criticism as "that thing we do that we cannot speak of directly." Even courses in critical theory tend to reduce the subject either to a version of the history of ideas or to a series of alternate methods for reading literary texts. Few such courses give primary attention to critical texts as texts in their own right—to their internal verbal structures, to the economics of their production, or to the atmosphere of individual uncertainty and vision in which they were composed. All this leads me back again to my main topic—the psychology of criticism. It may be useful to consider as self-defining the general absence of discourse about criticism. Part of the psychology of criticism is the very tendency to deny that its psychology exists.

We are all aware that this silence has been invaded repeatedly during the last few years, but it is important not to exaggerate the amount of attention critics have recently given to their enterprise. Serious analysis of the critical activity remains infrequent. Curiously enough, very few psychoanalytic critics have worked in this area, although their contribution could be considerable.[1] In any case, anyone who writes about the practice of criticism will be unable to ignore the tradition of *omerta* that surrounds the topic.

Silence surrounds not only general attitudes toward criticism but also the individual sentences of critical essays. A significant part of academic literary criticism amounts to the careful translation of individual experience into language that can be communally credited by the profession. This is partly an instance of a larger psychological necessity, one that Kenneth Burke describes succinctly: "I worked out a way of getting along by dodges, the main one being a concern with tricks whereby I could translate my self-involvements into speculations about 'people' in general."[2] In criticism, such translation is mediated not only through other texts but also by professional constraints that require verbal adaptations not always pleasurable to a writer. To turn these adaptations, as Burke does, into forms of play, is to succeed in mastering your discourse at the very moment you disavow it. For many critics, however, particularly inexperienced ones, these translations may feel more like repression and self-negation.

The sense of what is permissible, of what can be said, varies from field to field and from journal to journal. It undergoes constant change and is never wholly fixed in any case. Moreover, it depends in part upon who the person is, what his reputation is, and precisely what his previous work has led his audience to expect. Nonetheless, a rough consensus about the kind of discourse that is admissible does obtain at any moment in time. To violate these norms might seem to risk the standard kinds of professional excommunication. But genuine violation of these norms may be impossible, since what critics can know (and say) is a function of the critical languages available to them. These languages establish the terms of and the limits to any rupture that can take place within them, a constraint that must, of course, apply to the present topic as well.

An example from my own work may help to demonstrate how these pressures can function in a critical text. Several years ago I was writing about Milton's fascination with physical rigidity as a manifestation of a character's resistance to temptation. As my work progressed, I concentrated on *Paradise Regained*, keeping in mind the evidence for Milton's interest in inflexible physical postures at key points in his other works, but leaving it out of my essay. I wanted to end the essay with an epiphanic reading of Christ's posture at the conclusion of *Paradise Regained*. I wished to evoke the implicit sexuality of the scene and to connect that sexuality with the poem's religious vision. My final sentences read: "Christ's crucified body is the vehicle through which the seed of Eve will be planted in heaven. Symbolically the poem points the fallen reader in the direction of paradise. Its final posture: Christ standing at the still center of the turning world—a stone phallus in the womb of nature." This passage has served as a kind of red flag for its readers, several of whom have found it indecorous, irrational, or absurd. When Murray Schwartz reviewed the book of which the *Paradise Regained* essay is a chapter, he singled the passage out as a case when the author "seems so determined to find transcendent unity in the image of the body that he transforms his subject into the form of his desire."[3]

I think it is fair to say that much of the paraphrasable content of my paragraph could have been rendered in a form more acceptable to members of the profession. My style would have to be more discursive, less aphoristic. I would need to distance myself from the sense of apocalyptic participation communicated by my rhetoric; there are other kinds of enraptured exemplification that can serve similar emotional functions for the critic, while his readers find them more tolerable. Then I would need to reintroduce reasonably elaborate substantiation through Milton's other poems. Finally, I might allude to Jacques Lacan's analyses of the symbolic primacy of the phallus, so as to give my observations an external theoretical ground.

This sanitized, argumentative version of my paragraph would hardly be the same as the orginal. Yet my essential point—that similar insights become acceptable or unacceptable according to the language in which they are couched—remains unchanged. Though it does not negate Schwartz's point about my psychological motivation, it complicates it. What I wrote is arguably linked to Milton's text. Yet it is entirely relevant to ask what needs were served by my writing about the text in this particular way. The passage is not an instance of sheer subjectivity—if indeed such a thing exists—and an account of its psychology needs to treat all its components—textual, professional, and personal. Finally, it might be most fruitful to use the passage as a way of beginning to talk about the psychology of more prosaic portions of the essay. We need, in short, to be careful about how we privilege what seem to be overt admissions of a critic's own presence.

At least some of what I am saying here is common knowledge, but it is also largely unspoken knowledge. We all, no doubt, have had practice in negotiating between our individual experience and the consensus language of our particular fields. We recognize, at least in reading our own work, that its sentences record that kind of continual mediation. We know that mediation to be part of the substance of the critical activity, yet we remain largely silent about its effect on our own work and on that of others. For me, the satisfaction of writing criticism grows partly out of feeling that I am working at the edge of the state of consensus in my field, at the boundary where self-expression is brought forward, qualified, and brought forward again.

Let me try to identify a reasonably clear case of this kind of consensus in progress. At the end of a recent essay titled "Literary Theory: A Compass for Critics," Paul Hernadi writes "Practically everything I have said about texts in the foregoing pages also applies to the present essay. This means that you may wish to challenge the perspective or attitude of its implied author or else psychoanalyze its actual author and even reveal the socioeconomic motivation of his approach to literary theory."[4] One reason I was struck by this passage was that I had recently included a similar gesture in an essay titled "Reading Criticism." Hernadi and I acknowledged the self-relexive component of what we had written. Neither of us chose to go back and draw frequent attention to that level of our writing. Even as a gesture, however, it has its satisfactions. First, it is a form of decorous confession. Second, it provides at least some defense against just that objection's being raised against the essay. Yet it is not merely shyness or humility that limited how far either of us pursued the issue. One may counter that we rejected a continual and overt self-reflection because we knew our readers would find it intrusive or boring. That may be true, but their boredom would be both consensually determined and defensive. It cannot be the case that self-reflection is somehow ontologically boring; it is potentially as subject to rhetorical management and interest as any other form of discourse. Yet I would argue that as of 1976 such a brief comment was the permissible limit for acknowledged self-reflexive meditation in published critical theory. You will have no trouble finding other evidence to support this contention. Take, for example, Norman Holland's statement in *5 Readers Reading*, "my interpretations must necessarily express my own identity theme," or Harold Bloom's admission that his theory of influence is offered "in the context of his own anxieties of influence."[5] Neither Holland nor Bloom deals very effectively with the implications of their observations, though Holland makes a more serious effort than almost anyone else. For Bloom, of course, it is one proclamation among many. That in itself, however, is significant. While most critics would draw special attention to such moments—placing them strategically, using the first person and altering their tone, or making the point with obvious nervousness—Bloom's uniformly intense rhetoric makes it very difficult to privilege explicit self-reflection.

Now that I have called your attention to this small feature of the rhetoric of recent criticism, you may be inclined to dismiss it as mere rhetoric. Actually, I do not think that can ever quite be the case. Even if a critic merely appends such a comment as an afterthought, it will still reveal an awareness of the self-reflexive quality of critical writing and perhaps suggest both pleasure and uneasiness in that awareness. Such self-recognition, even when it is belated, contributes to the psychology of critical writing. At the same time, only the surrounding critical climate makes such self-awareness possible, permissible, and even probable. The consensus about acknowledged self-awareness in criticism is presently a highly unstable one. The critics I have cited here are, in effect, testing that consensus at the same time as they are testing themselves against their own work. Moreover, the rough consensus within the field of critical theory about how much self-recognition is possible and what forms it should take does not at all apply to the reactions of the profession as a whole, which responds according to my earlier model: self-consciousness is "silenced" as the nonsensical or the forbidden. Recent comments by Gerald Graff and Donald Reiman, among others, give sufficient voice to how the silent majority feels.[6]

Although these reactions are predictable, they are nonetheless helpful. As long as they actually appear in print, even if they are merely sarcastic or incensed, they create an atmosphere of debate and curiosity. The profession really has only two tactics it can use successfully against discourse that it rejects: not to publish it at all, or, having published it, to ignore it. Someone who feels compelled to deal with you has given you the only audience you need. Moreover, the presence of the nonsensical and the forbidden are always signs that the discourse between them can change. That is precisely the use that Bloom's criticism has for the profession. His theory of influence may never be widely adopted, but the reviews his books have received are changing the nature of what can be said. His publications have helped to open the discussion of literary critics to issues previously excluded.

None of this makes our questions about the psychology of criticism easier to resolve. My intention is rather to make a two-fold claim: first, for the necessity of considering the psychology of criticism, and second, for the necessity of considering its continual relativity. I can think of no better way to emphasize the second point than by examining for a moment the recent work of the critic who has argued perhaps most visibly that literary interpretation is shaped by our individual psychology, Norman Holland.

Holland's recent work regularly includes characterizations of his own identity theme, which he feels governs both his relations to literary texts and his habitual critical stances. "For me," he writes, "the need to see and understand is very strong." "I feel a real conflict in me between scientific impulses and literary ones." He has "a passionate desire to know about the insides of things with an equally strong feeling that one is, finally, safer on the outside." For that reason, he writes, "I *like* examining the verbal surface of a text, looking particularly for an 'organic unity' in the way the parts all come together."[7] As I read Holland's list, I find myself somewhat alienated by his cheerful form of self-presentation; it is not my style. Except for that, however, I have little difficulty in reciting his personal characteristics in the first person. Indeed, it would be curious if I did have trouble doing so, for these qualities are commonplace features of virtually any critical writing. They are, in short, unrevealing and impersonal; in different ways we can all assent to them. Perhaps we are intended to, thereby congratulating ourselves at how harmless and unthreatening psychoanalysis has proven to be and, of course, accepting Holland's theory, since we can presumably credit these as our identity themes as well. These decorous, sanitized statements of the will to power are designed, perhaps unconsciously, to offer only the most minimal challenge to the current consensus about the motives for interpretation. Compare another version: "My identity theme [has] to do with preserving a sense of self and securing self-esteem by gaining power over relations between things, in particular, mastering them by knowing or seeing them from outside rather than being actually in the relationships." The next sentence is the crucial one: "Not a bad hang-up, if you want to be a literary critic."[8] These are, as I have argued, conventional critical "hang-ups."

The identity themes I have just cited could actually have been presented with double sets of quotation marks, since they are now so codified for Holland that he offers them as self-quotation from his previous work. This pattern of self-quotation has two interesting effects. First, it gives his original speculation about his identity theme a retroactive evidentiary status, although that status is unconvincing and thus slightly comic. Second, the quotation marks give the material a fixed and immutable status; it need not be confronted or considered any further. Holland tends to place this cluster of identity themes at the end of his essays. The reader encountering the list for the first time comes to it expecting Holland to conclude with dramatic self-revelation and thus feels rather cheated. Yet perhaps there *is* more than a consensual code here. The persona Holland most often puts forward in his criticism is convincingly open, generous, and even innocent. If Holland has a sense of self-exposure and cleansing confession when he writes about his desire for power, perhaps it is because such a motive, however commonplace, is so remote from the voice he has already established in his criticism. Nonetheless, these statements of his identity theme are so formulaic that they block any extended exploration of the guilt critics usually feel when they recognize, however obliquely, their wish to reconstruct a text and reorder it in their minds. There are hints of that in Holland's very enthusiasm. There are also suggestions, elsewhere in his work, of how his perspective does differ from that of the profession as a whole. Earlier in one of these essays he reports that he feels "punished" by the second stanza of Wordsworth's "A Slumber did my Spirit Seal."[9] That is a more curious and indeed more intimate reaction than those he reports in his official identity themes, and it shows that Holland can, when he wants, risk himself in his writing in ways most critics still resist.

In this sketch of some of the tensions in Holland's criticism, we see how it is possible to talk about the psychology of a particular critic's writing by testing it against the general psychology of criticism. There is rarely need, I would argue, to resort to biographical information in order to write about the psychology of most critics' work. What is essential now is to begin looking at critical texts themselves with some sensitivity to the psychology of their rhetoric. The goal is to elucidate the psychology of what has been written and thereby to read critical texts in a more informed and humanly plausible way, not to use critical texts as a way of reconstructing personal histories. I make that point not only in order to reassure those who are concerned about standards for professional interaction but also to emphasize the centrality of the critical texts themselves, as opposed to any information we can bring to them. I am not offering this dictum so as to privilege these texts in the New Critical sense, but merely to draw attention to language that critics have so far not been reading and discussing with sufficient care. One does, however, need to know the intellectual and cultural milieu in which a critic worked. Such matters as a critic's terminology or the tone he takes toward his contemporaries may be inexplicable or misleading without that information. Where more personal biographical evidence seems relevant, its use should be governed by the same standards for the passage of time that apply in discussions of poetry or fiction.

Actually, an inquiry into the psychology of criticism is an almost inevitable outgrowth of any effort to read and reread criticism as thoroughly as poetry and fiction. A first reading of a criticial text might at best be comparable to reading a novel with complete absorption in its plot. Since we are more resistant to the literary properties of critical essays, we are likely to read them with even less sensitivity than that. As we reread a critical essay, however, or as we read a series of essays in which the same critic treats different texts, we are more likely to recognize those recurring metaphors and controlling verbal structures that typify a particular critic's work. As soon as we recognize a critic's own intellectual interests and rhetorical styles, they will be foregrounded when we read his prose. At that point the critic becomes a writer and the need to attend to psychological effect and motivation is apparent. In arguing that changing our reading habits would change what we feel to be appropriate and necessary to say about critical languages, I am, of course, aware that our present reading habits reinforce (and perhaps grow out of) the disinclination to discuss criticism in more human and literary terms.

My own thinking about the usefulness of psychological and psychoanalytic readings of critical texts has changed over the past few years. I first argued that psychoanalytic categories would prove too reductive to account for complex critical prose. Then I decided that psychoanalysis would be useful in reading critical texts that displayed fantasy material substantially unrelated to the primary texts discussed. In the first case, I had in mind works like Northrop Frye's *Anatomy of Criticism*. Would it be useful, I wondered, when Frye writes that criticism can show that all literature coheres in a single body, to assert that this reconstituted body is the body of the mother? Would

it be useful to say of all interpreted texts, all texts reconstructed through critical meditation, that such texts are always the
reconstituted mother? I have since decided that such generali-
zations are useful, that they provide a reductive challenge that
can help us to see how critics work to avoid those very recogni-
tions as they write. Sophisticated critical language cannot be
dismissed by tracing its psychological motivation or by establishing its connection with primary psychoanalytic metaphors,
but its tensions can be illuminated in that way. Just as many
critics fear the sentimental and romantic components of their
intellection, so too do many critics struggle against the motivational core of their work. The interest of criticism's elaborate
verbal strategies can actually be intensified by the very reductive force that psychoanalytic language can exercise on these
motivations. Nonetheless, initial reactions to this reductive
challenge will not be positive. Indeed, I am reminded of the
history of reactions to Kenneth Burke's infamous suggestion
that Keats's most well-known line can also be read "Body is
turd, turd body." Burke's later comment on his notion suggests
as well how critics often deal with self-knowledge as they write:
"Any such bathos," Burke writes, "lurking behind the poem's
pathos, is so alien to the formal pretenses of the work, if such
indecorous transliterating of the poem's decorum had occurred
to Keats, in all likelihood he would have phrased his formula
differently, to avoid this turn."[10] This kind of disguise and
sublimation is essential to the psychology of criticism, especially as that psychology reflects the profession's consensus
about what can and cannot be said in critical writing.

   In terms of its object relations, criticism as we have agreed
to practice it in America is grounded in a communal sense of
how readers may and may not internalize the texts they discuss.
In psychoanalytic language, we can say that the standards for
object relations in criticism demand a distinction between introjection and incorporation. These would not, of course, be terms

many critics would use to describe their enterprise. They do, however, reflect one assumption to which many of us would assent, namely, that criticism is always constituted *as* a relationship, since neither reader nor text can literally be subsumed by the other.

The history of introjection and incorporation in psychoanalytic literature has left the terms closely related, with their differences often indistinct. Both terms refer to the process whereby we transfer objects from outside to inside the self. Incorporation, however, has usually been a more narrow term, linked with a bodily model that is always potentially reducible to orality. Introjection is usually a broader term, growing out of its bodily prototype but referring widely to all the ways in which a subject internalizes objects psychically. Nonetheless, some writers prefer the use of incorporation, since it emphasizes the physical basis of the ego. In any case, the two terms typically describe a matrix of object relations; if not interchangeable, they are at least complementary. There has, however, been some effort to bring these terms into more active confrontation, particularly in the work of Nicolas Abraham and Maria Torok. Jacques Derrida's discussion, in his essay "Fors," of the implications of their efforts to redefine introjection and incorporation can provide a useful model of American criticism's essential ambivalence toward the object relations it enacts.[11]

Abraham and Torok treat introjection and incorporation almost as opposite modes of internalization. Introjection, as they define it, involves a more thorough assimilation of the object. The subject does not completely identify with the introjected object, but the object now includes the instincts and desires attached to it. Incorporation, on the other hand, provides a rather different form of internalization. The object is internalized but unintegrated. It is included within the self, but alien to it, inaccessible; in effect, to use Derrida's language, it is "enclosed, entombed, encysted inside the Self."[12] Incorporation provides a surprisingly apt analogy for the special, privileged status we assign to the literary text and to the form of internalization we know as interpretation. In criticism, the encrypted object is the interpreted text.

It is probably fair to say that all readers share some desire to have the text completely introjected. All of us, then, may partly wish to encounter the text as though the ego were encountering its own symbolic objects. Yet that wish also reflects a desire for change, and, indeed, in the process of internalizing a text we may feel for a moment that the self we brought to the encounter has actually been reshaped. The profession, however, insists that we opt instead for incorporation, defined as a way of keeping the text separate and inaccessible while nonetheless within the self. The interpreted text, like the encrypted object, is "the vault of a desire," containing it, representing it, while simultaneously pretending to deny it. Incorporation, or interpretation, "negotiates clandestinely with a prohibition it neither accepts nor transgresses." Interpretation, like incorporation, "is a kind of theft to reappropriate the pleasure-object."[13] Thus the negotiations between the idealized, hypostatized text and the text as a matrix of our own desires can never be truly curtailed. Convincingly written criticism requires a familiarity with the text that must move through introjection to draw on moments of near identification. Indeed, for some critics, especially phenomenological critics like Georges Poulet or Gaston Bachelard, a condition like introjection, when the text reoccurs within the critic's first-person discourse, constitutes an interpretive goal. In the New Critical tradition, however, such successful integration must be rhetorically posited as separation and distance; these hierophantic readings can speak of but not within the text's miraculous enclosure and inner self-sufficiency. Criticism then must show that the text is encrypted within the self. The text's announced, official status is its privileged incorporation; its secret condition is introjection. For much of

American criticism, we may say, modifying Abraham and Torok, that the fantasy of incorporation disguises the process of introjection. This model, however, is entirely reversible; those critics who urge us to adopt complete introjection as a critical procedure also inescapably engage in acts of incorporation. They may tend, for example, to privilege, to hypostatize, and finally to encrypt the special site on which they imagine their own consciousness merges with that of the author they discuss. One can never, therefore, actually choose one or the other mode of internalization: "Introjection/incorporation: everything is played out on the borderline which divides and opposes the two terms."[14] Criticism records our efforts to negotiate between those two modes of relation. To examine how critics do that when they write is only to read them and speak of them more frankly.

To seek the truth about the psychology of criticism is not to denigrate the field or to risk its losing ground in competition with other fields whose pretenses to objectivity are more secure. In a time when the humanities are notoriously in crisis, perhaps we have more to gain by exploiting the very vulnerability of literary criticism as a mode of inquiry. If criticism is distinguished among the humanities in no other way, it is at least distinguished by the very bulk of its output over the past thirty years. If we can consider this body of discourse —in its very disparate collectivity—as a representative form of human knowledge, then at least it will not appear from the outside as gratuitous accumulation. Yet we need to deal with our own resistance to the project and we cannot do that without beginning to read and write about criticism in such a way as to open discussion of its psychology. When we restore to criticism a sense of the doubt, ambition, and vision that its sentences record, we will not find its human features to be unique or destructive.

The polemical energy of this essay is directed, then, not at

60   Cary Nelson

the psychology of critics but at the prohibition against discussing their psychology. I would urge toward the work of individual critics not greater aggression but a more meticulous empathy.
To enter into a critic's works, attempting to live in that world,
eliciting the motivation structured into and compromised by
individual sentences, describing the satisfaction and deception
in large verbal structures—all this requires the same intimacy
we experience with novelists and poets. This seems to me to
be the special contribution that psychology and psychoanalysis
can now make to the study of criticism. Does criticism have a
psychology? Yes. Let this be thought, let it be written.

NOTES

This paper is one of a series of essays I have written on the literary status of critical
discourse. See "The Paradox of Critical Language: A Polemical Speculation," *MLN*
89 (1974): 1003-16; "Reading Criticism," *PMLA* 91 (1976): 801-15; "Letter to the
Forum," *PMLA* 92 (1977): 310-12; "Allusion and Authority: Hugh Kenner's Exemplary Critical Voice," *Denver Quarterly* 12, 1 (1977): 282-95. The present essay was
completed with the assistance of an appointment at the University of Illinois Center
for Advanced Study.

1. Although there is no lack of psychoanalytic studies of fiction and poetry, there
are very few psychoanalytic studies of nonfiction prose of any kind. In that context,
see Loyd S. Pettegrew, "Psychoanalytic Theory: A Neglected Rhetorical Dimension,"
Philosophy and Rhetoric 10 (1977): 46-59. This failure to give sufficient attention
to the psychology of rhetorical discourse reinforces the ironic absence of method-
ological self-awareness and reflection in most psychoanalytic literary criticism.

2. Kenneth Burke, "Dancing with Tears in My Eyes," *Critical Inquiry* 1 (1974): 26.

3. Murray Schwartz, review of *The Incarnate Word: Literature as Verbal Space*
(Urbana: University of Illinois Press, 1973), in *Criticism* 17 (1975): 187-89.

4. Paul Hernadi, "Literary Theory: A Compass for Critics," *Critical Inquiry* 3
(1976): 369-86.

5. Norman Holland, *5 Readers Reading* (New Haven: Yale University Press, 1975),
p. 66; Harold Bloom, *The Anxiety of Influence* (New York: Oxford University Press,
1973), p. 12.

6. Gerald Graff, "Fear and Trembling at Yale," *The American Scholar* (1977),
467-78; Donald Reiman, "Letter to the Forum," *PMLA* 92 (1977): 309.

7. Norman Holland, "Literary Interpretation and Three Phases of Psychoanalysis,"
Critical Inquiry 3 (1976): 221-33.

8. Norman Holland, "Transactive Criticism: Re-Creation Through Identity,"
Criticism 18 (1976): 334-52.

9. Holland, "Literary Interpretation," p. 222.

10. Kenneth Burke, "As I Was Saying," *Michigan Quarterly Review* 11, 1 (1972): 22. For the background to (and somewhat hesitant development of) Burke's notorious "joycing" of Keats's poem, see "Symbolic Action in a Poem by Keats," appended to *A Grammar of Motives* (New York: Prentice-Hall, 1945; subsequently reprinted by Braziller, Meridian Books, and the University of California Press), and *A Rhetoric of Motives* (New York: Prentice-Hall, 1950, reprinted as above), p. 204, where Burke provides a linguistic equation that the reader can use to obtain the formula that seemed unprintable at the time.

11. Jacques Derrida, "Fors," *Georgia Review* 31 (1977): 64-120.

12. Ibid., p. 70.

13. Ibid., p. 72.

14. Ibid., p. 70.

Neil Hertz

The Notion of Blockage
in the Literature of the Sublime

There is, according to Kant, a sense of the sublime—he calls it the mathematical sublime—arising out of sheer cognitive exhaustion, the mind blocked not by the threat of an overwhelming force, but by the fear of losing count or of being reduced to nothing but counting—this and this and this—with no hope of bringing a long series or a vast scattering under some sort of conceptual unity. Kant describes a painful pause—"a momentary checking of the vital powers"—followed by a compensatory positive movement, the mind's exultation in its own rational faculties, in its ability to think a totality that cannot be taken in through the senses.[1] In illustration, Kant alludes to "the bewilderment or, as it were, perplexity which it is said seizes the spectator on his first entrance into St. Peter's at Rome,"[2] but one needn't go to Rome to experience bewilderment or perplexity. They are available in quantity much closer to home. Professional explainers of literature have only to try to locate themselves in the current intellectual scene, to try to determine what is to be learned from the linguists or the philosophers or the psychoanalysts or the political economists, in order to experience the requisite mental overload, and possibly even that momentary checking of the vital powers. It is difficult to speculate about literature just now without sounding either more assured or more confused than one really feels. In such circumstances, some remarks about the mathematical sublime, that is, about one version of the play between confusion and assurance, might prove useful. In particular, it may be useful to examine that moment of blockage, the "checking of the vital powers," to consider both the role it played in eighteenth- and nineteenth-century accounts of the sublime and the fascination it still seems to exert on contemporary historians and theorists of literature.

THE FLOOD OF PUBLICATION

Consider first some paragraphs from a recent issue of *Studies in English Literature*;[3] they express a scholar's fear that soon we shall all be overwhelmed by the rising tide of academic publication. The genre of this writing may be that of the omnibus review (Thomas McFarland is here reporting on a year's worth of literary studies), but tonally and thematically it can be grouped with the last lines of *The Dunciad*, with the "Analytic of the Sublime," or with Wordsworth's dream of the Arab bearing the emblems of culture just ahead of "the fleet waters of a drowning world."

First, the threat represented by the dimensions of the problem:

> It is not simply that there is no one—such is the exponential accumulation of secondary discussion—who can any longer claim to be competent to provide specialist commentary on more than a decade or two . . .; it is, more complexly, that the burgeoning contributions call into question the use and purpose of culture as such. Just as the enormous increase in human population threatens all the values of individuality so carefully inculcated by centuries of humanistic refinement, so too does the flood of publication threaten the very knowledge that publication purports to serve.

Notice that the population explosion is not brought into the argument literally, as yet another problem (one with a certain world-historical urgency of its own), but figuratively, as a thrilling comparison, a current topos of the mathematical sublime. We might suspect that other figures of scary proliferation may be at hand, and indeed they are:

> What then will be the eventual disposition and use of most of these secondary studies? The answer seems clear: in due course their contents

will be programmed into a computer, and, as time passes, will more and more be remembered by the computer and forgotten by men. And in a still further length of time, it will be possible not only to reproduce instantaneously any aspect of previous secondary work, but actually to produce new work simply by instructing the computer to make the necessary recombinations. The wheel will then have come full circle: computers will be writing for computers, and the test of meaningful publication will be to think and write in a way a computer could not.

Certain turns of phrase—the fine Johnsonian cadence of "remembered by the computer and forgotten by men," for example—suggest that McFarland may have taken a mournful pleasure in working up this fragment of science fiction, but we may suspect that he's also quite serious: this is something more than a reviewer's ritual groan. In fact, the statement of the problem is accompanied by a rapid and pointed analysis of its causes. McFarland sees that the justification for much scholarly activity is itself a fiction; one pretends a work is "needed" on, say, Shelley's life; in truth, as McFarland notes, "the need goes the other way. The student needs the doctorate; then needs an academic position; then needs recognition and advancement." Critical and scholarly writing proliferates as the energies of personal ambition are fed into an increasingly unwieldy and mindless institutional machine.

If one agrees with McFarland's analysis and shares his dismay, one reads on with certain ethical or political expectations, imagining that one is about to be told what ought to be done, or perhaps one is about to see something being done right then and there—the reviewer savagely but righteously clearing the field of at least a few unnecessary books. In fact, nothing of the sort develops. What follows this intense and, I assume, earnest indictment is a summary of nineteenth-century studies that is distinguished by its critical intelligence and knowledgeability but is not in any other way out of the ordinary. It is written with a great deal of generosity and with no signs whatever that its writer is anything but content with his role: he has made a

professional commitment to review these books and he is carry-
ing it out in a professional fashion.

We seem to have come a long way from the mathematical sublime, but I believe we are still very much within its field of force.
We have simple followed the reviewer to a point of blockage: he
has written of the threat of being overwhelmed by too much
writing, and it may not be possible to go beyond that—in writing. The appropriate corrective measures may still be taken elsewhere, and we can assume McFarland knows what they are: in
his dealings with his students and colleagues, in the pressure he
applies on publishers and on the makers of university and foundation and government policy, he can still wield varying degrees
of influence on the politics of literary scholarship. If he nevertheless sounds thwarted, it may not be chiefly because the dimensions of the political problem are out of proportion to his
own practical force, but rather because he has run his expression of his sense of the problem to the point where he can
glimpse another sort of incommensurability. That, at least, is
what I gather from another paragraph in the review, one that
may be read as a gesture beyond blockage, but that produces
only a further occasion for bewilderment:

> The scholar, in Emerson's conception, is "man thinking." With the pro-
> liferation of secondary comment, he must necessarily become ever more
> something else: man reading. And yet, in a very real sense the whole
> aim of culture should be the integration of awareness—should be even-
> tually to read less, not more. "The constant influx of other people's
> ideas," writes Schopenhauer, "must certainly stop and stifle our own,
> and indeed, in the long run paralyze the power of thought. . . . There-
> fore incessant reading and study positively ruin the mind. . . . Reading
> no longer anticipates thinking, but entirely takes its place."

In the face of "the proliferation of secondary comment"—
plural, heterogeneous, dismaying—the reviewer posits an ideal,
"the integration of awareness," and the human, if abstract,
embodiment of that ideal, the figure of "man thinking." But if
McFarland would enjoin us, and himself, to read less, not more,

why has he gone on to cite Schopenhauer, when Schopenhauer is saying much the same thing that he has just thoughtfully set down himself? Why wasn't once enough, especially for someone who is insisting that enough is enough?

I don't think a serious answer to that question can be framed either in terms of personal psychology or in terms of institutional structures: those vocabularies of motivation have been left behind by the language of that paragraph. Its rhetorical heightening (its invocation of Emerson and Schopenhauer, the urgency we hear in phrases like "in a very real sense") its insistence that thinking is to be distinguished from reading just when, paradoxically, it is displaying what looks like an unavoidable contamination of the one by the other—all this suggests that the reviewer has led us, willy-nilly, into the region of the sublime. In a scenario characteristic of the sublime, an attempt to come to terms with plurality in the interest of an "integration of awareness" has generated a curiously spare tableau: the mind blocked in confrontation with an unsettling and indeterminate play between two elements (here called "man thinking" and "man reading") that themselves resist integration. We can better understand the logic of this scenario if we turn back to some of its earlier manifestations.

THE "CONFUSED SEAS OF ENGLISH THEORIES OF THE SUBLIME"

The moment of blockage is a familiar one to readers of Wordsworth, who repeatedly represents himself as, in his phrasing, "thwarted, baffled and rescued in his own despite,"[4] halted and checked in some activity—sometimes clearly perverse, sometimes apparently innocuous—then released into another order of experience or of discourse: the Simplon Pass episode and the encounter with the Blind Beggar are but two of the most memorable of such passages in *The Prelude*. If the experience seems to us both very Wordsworthian and perfectly natural, that may be in part a tribute to the persuasiveness of Wordsworth's poetry, in part a way of acknowledging how commonplace the scenario (if not the experience) had become by the end of the eighteenth century. Kant's "Analytic of the Sublime" (1790) offers the most rigorous philosophical account, but the staging of blockage had been blocked out much earlier. Samuel Monk finds it already informing Addison's description of the imagination's pleasurable dealings with greatness, "its aspiration to grasp the object, the preordained failure, and the consequent feeling of bafflement, and the sense of awe and wonder."[5] "Various men," Monk comments, "were to use this pattern with varying significance, but it is essentially the sublime experience from Addison to Kant." In fact, it was his noticing the continuity of this pattern that allowed Monk to organize his history of what he refers to as the "chaos" of esthetic speculation in the eighteenth century. His book opens with a careful paraphrase of Kant because, as he says, "it would be unwise to embark on the confused seas of English theories of the sublime without having some ideas as to where we are going";[6] it concludes with a long citation from the Sixth Book of *The Prelude*—the lines on the Simplon Pass— which Monk reads as the "apotheosis" of the eighteenth-century sublime.

Because the task of the historian—the reduction to narrative order of a large, sometimes seemingly infinite mass of detail—resembles the play of apprehension and comprehension, of counting and organizing, associated with the mathematical sublime, it might be worth dwelling for a moment on Monk's introductory remarks about his history. "Theories of beauty," he writes, "are relatively trim and respectable; but in theories of the sublime one catches the century somewhat off its guard, sees it, as it were, without powder or pomatum, whalebone and patches." What people are led to call "chaos" sometimes strikes them as the confused seas on which they must embark; here, in a figure equally traditional, chaos is a woman out of Swift or Rowlandson, in disarray and déshabille, slightly all over the place, not yet fit to be seen. There is a *soupçon* of blockage

about this fondly misogynistic turn, but Monk's mind soon recuperates its powers and reestablishes its forward movement:
"Indeed, the chief problem has been the problem of organiza-
tion. The necessity of imposing form of some sort has continually led to the danger of imposing a false or artificial form." If
raw heterogeneity—the world without whalebone and patches—
is a danger, so is sheer willfully cosmetic unity, "artificial form";
we are led to expect an image of synthesis or integration, and
we are not disappointed: "I have therefore grouped the theories
together loosely under very general headings in an effort to indicate that there is a progress, slow and continuous, but that this
progress is one of organic growth. . . . The direction of this
growth is toward the subjectivism of Kant."[7]

Monk's book was written over forty years ago, when historians of eighteenth-century literature and philosophy were not
afraid of using the word "preromanticism" or of picturing the
century teleologically, as if it were en route to writers like
Wordsworth or Kant, or to concepts like that of the Imagination. That mode of historical argument has been sufficiently
challenged so that Monk's narrative may seem dated. Yet the
most recent comprehensive theoretical study of the sublime, a
splendidly intelligent book by Thomas Weiskel,[8] still finds its
organizing figures in Kant and Wordsworth, and more particularly, in their accounts of the mind's movement, blockage, and
release. Is the moment of blockage, then, simply a *fact* about
the experience of the sublime, attested to by one after another
eighteenth-century writer, available for the subsequent general-
izing commentary of historians like Monk or literary theorists
like Weiskel? I think not; rather, a look at the provenance of the
notion of blockage will reveal a more interesting development.

Eighteenth-century writers do not use the word "blockage";
they use verbs like "baffle" and "check" or nouns like "aston-
ishment" or "difficulty." Here, for example, is Hume on the
reason we venerate "the relicts of antiquity"; "The mind, ele-

vated by the vastness of its object, is still farther elevated by the difficulty of the conception; and being oblig'd every moment to renew its efforts in the transition from one part of time to another, feels a more vigorous and sublime disposition."[9] "Difficulty," Hume had just written, "instead of extinguishing [the mind's] vigour and alacrity, has the contrary effect, of sustaining and encreasing it." Language such as this—and there is much similar talk throughout the century of the tonic effects of opposition or sheer recalcitrance—language such as this is easily enough assimilated to the pattern of motion and blockage, but it is worth noticing that it is not saying quite the same thing: here the mind is braced and roused but not absolutely (even if only for a moment) checked. This may sound trivial, a mere difference in degree, but such differences, between the absolute and the not-so-absolute, often take on philosophical and narrative importance. When Saul, on his way to Damascus, was thwarted, baffled, and rescued in his own despite, the Bible does not report that he merely faltered in his purpose, slumped to his hands and knees, then rose at the count of nine. The example can serve as a reminder that the metaphor of blockage draws much of its power from the literature of religious conversion, that is, from a literature that describes major experiential transformation, the mind not merely challenged and thereby invigorated but thoroughly "turned round."

As for the notion of difficulty, Angus Fletcher has shown that it too has a religious origin, although it is associated not with the act of conversion but with the more commonplace—and continuous—activity of interpreting the figurative language of Scripture, of working out the sense of what had come to be known as "difficult ornament." I quote from Fletcher's discussion in his book on allegory:

> "Difficulty" implies here a calculated obscurity which elicits an interpretive response in the reader. The very obscurity is a source of pleasure, especially to the extent that the actual process of deciphering the

exegetical content of a passage would be painfully arduous and uncertain. Obscurity stirs curiosity; the reader wants to tear the veil aside. "The more they seem obscure through their use of figurative expressions," says Augustine, "the more they give pleasure when they have been made clear."[10]

The citation of Augustine can remind us that discussions of religious conversion and of Biblical exegesis are not entirely irrelevant to one another, the intermediate notion, as Fletcher indicates, being that of an ascesis of reading:

Augustine is pointing to a cosmic uncertainty embodied in much of Scripture, in response to which he can only advocate an interpretive frame of mind, which for him becomes the occasion for an *ascesis*. The mixture of pain and pleasure, an intellectual tension accompanying the hard work of exegetical labor, is nothing less than the cognitive aspect of the ambivalence which inheres in the contemplation of any sacred object. Whatever is *sacer* must cause the shiver of mingled delight and awe that constitutes our sense of "difficulty."

Augustinian ascesis organizes reading so that it becomes a movement, albeit with difficult steps, down the line toward a pleasure that is not merely pleasure but also a guarantee of the proximity of the sacred object. I think we can find an equivalent of that in the eighteenth century's absorption of the rhetorical concept of difficulty into the experiential notion of blockage. This process is contemporary with the progressive loss of interest in Longinus's treatise, or rather, with the selective appropriation of elements of his rhetoric as modes of extraliterary experience. The two processes would seem to go together, although in ways I have not yet made clear. The translation of "difficulty" into "blockage" and the submersion of the rhetorical sublime so that its figures function as a sort of experiential underwriting, both of these seem like strategies designed to consolidate a reassuringly operative notion of the self. A telling paragraph from an eclectic mid-century theorist, Alexander Gerard, can provide us with an illustration of the strategy at work:

> We always contemplate objects and ideas with a disposition similar to
> their nature. When a large object is presented, the mind expands itself
> to the extent of that object, and is filled with one grand sensation, which
> totally possessing it, composes it into a solemn sedateness, and strikes it
> with deep silent wonder and admiration: it finds such a difficulty in
> spreading itself to the dimensions of its object, as enlivens and invig-
> orates its frame: and having overcome the opposition which this occa-
> sions, it sometimes imagines itself present in every part of the scene
> which it contemplates; and from the sense of this immensity, feels a
> noble pride, and entertains a lofty conception of its own capacity.[11]

Notions of "difficulty" and "blockage" are loosely accommodated by this prose, which draws on Addison and Hume as well
as on Longinus. The mind, seeking to match itself to its object,
"expands," and that "enlivens" and "invigorates" it; but when
its capacity matches the extent of the object, the sense of containing the object, but also (with a hint of theological paradox)
of being filled by it, possessed by it, blocks the mind's further
movement and "composes it into a solemn sedateness," "strikes
it with deep silent wonder." The activity of the mind may be
associated with an enlivening sense of difficulty, but the mind's
unity is most strongly felt when it is "filled with one grand sensation," a container practically indistinguishable from the one
thing it contains; and it is precisely the mind's unity that is at
stake in such discussions of the natural sublime. The "integration of awareness" thus posited is achieved by a passage to the
limit that carries the notion of difficulty to the point where it
turns into absolute difficulty, a negative moment but nevertheless a reassuring one.

KANT, FREUD, AND THE MATHEMATICAL SUBLIME

Earlier, in considering Samuel Monk's introductory remarks,
I assumed an analogy between the scholar's imagining himself
heroically coming to grips with a chaotic heap of historical

matter and the situation of the hero of one of Kant's sublime scenarios, that of the mathematical sublime. I wish now to look a bit more closely at Kant's "Analytic of the Sublime," this time in connection with the work of another modern interpreter, Thomas Weiskel. It is Weiskel's distinction to have seen that the poetic and philosophic language of the primary sublime texts could be made to resonate with two quite different twentieth-century idioms, that of psychoanalysis and that of the semiological writings of Saussure, Jakobson, and Barthes. Weiskel's fine responsiveness to poetry, along with the patience and lucidity with which he elaborates a complex argument, make his book a difficult one to excerpt or to summarize, but my own understanding of the sublime requires me to come to terms with at least some elements of it, to question it at certain points and to explore the ways it locates itself in relation to its material. I shall be chiefly concerned with his discussion of the mathematical sublime, more particularly still with his attempt to bring Kant within the explanatory range of Freudian metapsychology.

Partly to satisfy the internal necessities of the Critical Philosophy, partly in response to an observable difference in accounts of sublime experience, Kant divides his consideration of the sublime into two sections, depending on whether the feeling is generated by the mind's confrontation with a seemingly overwhelming natural force (this is the dynamical sublime, the sublime of waterfalls, hurricanes, earthquakes, and the like) or else by the disturbances of cognition I described in the first section of this paper. This latter is the sublime of magnitude, the mathematical sublime, and it is of this mode that Kant writes: "For there is here a feeling of the inadequacy of [the] imagination for presenting the ideas of a whole, wherein the imagination reaches its maximum, and, in striving to surpass it, sinks back into itself, by which, however, a kind of emotional satisfaction is produced."[12] This is, one senses, the intellectual's sublime (Weiskel calls it, appropriately, the reader's or hermeneutical sublime). Kant is seemingly even-handed in his treatment of the two modes; he makes no attempt to subordinate the one to the other, but rather, he locates each in relation to the branching symmetries of his entire system. The mathematical sublime is associated with cognition and hence with the epistemological concerns of the *Critique of Pure Reason*; the dynamical sublime, because it confirms man's sense of his "spiritual destination," is referred to what Kant calls the faculty of desire and hence to the ethical concerns of the second *Critique*. But here an important qualification is introduced: the mathematical sublime too, it develops, shares this link with the ethical. For, as Kant presents this drama of collapse and compensation, the "emotional satisfaction" he finds there is taken to be an effect of the recognition that what the imagination has failed to bring into a unity (the infinite or the indefinitely plural) can nevertheless be *thought* as such, and that the agent of this thinking, the reason, must thus be a guarantor of man's "supersensible destiny." What is intriguing is that the drama seems to be available for two incompatible interpretations: we can think of it as the story of Ethics coming to the rescue in a situation of cognitive distress, or we can see that distress as slightly factitious, staged precisely in order to require the somewhat melodramatic arrival of Ethics. This is the sort of puzzle to which Weiskel addresses himself.

Weiskel's deliberate strategy is that of a translator. He would seek to understand the sublime by construing it, as he puts it, outside the presuppositions of idealism.[13] The drama of the imagination's collapse and reason's intervention, for example, looks like it might allow itself to be restaged in modern dress and in a psychoanalytic vernacular. The delight in the mathematical sublime, Kant had written, is a feeling of "imagination by its own act depriving itself of its freedom by receiving a final determination in accordance with a law other than that of its empirical employment." "In this way," Kant continues, "it gains an extension and a power greater than that which it sacrifices. But the ground of this is concealed from it, and in its place it *feels* the sacrifice or deprivation to which it is subjected." Weiskel cites the passage, then wonders at its motivational structure: why can't the imagination share the mind's pleasure in reason? why this talk of sacrifice and concealment? There is, further, he notices, a hint that the imagination has been, in a way, entrapped, led into this disaster by reason itself and for reason's own ends. "The real motive or cause of the sublime," Weiskel suggests, "is not efficient but teleological; we are ultimately referred not to the failure of empirical imagination but to reason's project in requiring this failure. The cause of the sublime is the *aggrandizement of reason at the expense of reality and the imaginative apprehension of reality*."[14]

Readers of Freud should have no trouble predicting the general direction of Weiskel's argument: the Kantian sublime, in both its manifestations, becomes for him "the very moment in which the mind turns within and performs its identification with reason. The sublime recapitulates and thereby reestablishes the oedipus complex," with Kant's reason taking the role of the superego, that agency generated by an act of sublimation, "an identification with the father taken as a model."[15]

What one could not have foreseen is the turn Weiskel's argument takes at this point. Throughout his discussion of the mathematical sublime, he has had to come to terms with the question of excess; for the theme of magnitude, of that which resists conceptualization, was bound to raise the problem. Until now, to the extent that both the mathematical and the dynamical sublime could be rendered as affirmative of reason— that is, of the superego—it had been possible to think of excess in terms of Freud's discussion of excessive identification, of that supererogatory strength of investment that turns the super-

ego into a harsher taskmaster than the father on whom it is
modeled. But there may be other forms of excess associated
with the mathematical sublime that are not so easily accounted
for: is it possible that there is excess that cannot, in Jacques
Derrida's phrase, be brought back home to the father? Weiskel
takes up the question in a section that begins with what sounds
like a scholar's twinge of conscience about his own sublime
operations of mind: "Have we not," he asks, "arrived at [this]
model by pressing one theory and suppressing a multitude of
facts for which it cannot account?" This qualm, intensified by a
further look at some lines from *The Prelude*, leads Weiskel to
suspect that the "anxiety of the sublime does not ultimately
result from the pressure of the super-ego after all . . . . that the
oedipus complex is not its deep structure."[16] What follows is an
intensely reasoned and difficult four pages, as Weiskel works to
integrate this new discovery into the larger movement of his
argument. This involves him in an exploration of the terrors
and wishes of the pre-oedipal phases, where he finally locates
the motivating power of the mathematical sublime, then sees
that as rejoining a secondary system that is recognizably oedipal
and more clearly manifested in the dynamical sublime. I quote
his conclusion:

> We should not be surprised to find that the sublime moment is over-
> determined in its effect on the mind. The excess which we have sup-
> posed to be the precipitating occasion, or "trigger", directly prompts
> the secondary anxiety in the case of the dynamical sublime of terror.
> In the mathematical sublime, however, the traumatic phase exhibits a
> primary system on which the secondary (guilt) system is superimposed.
> This situation explains an odd but unmistakable fact of Kant's analytic.
> Whenever he is generalizing about both versions of the negative sub-
> lime, the (secondary) rhetoric of power dominates. It is not logically
> necessary that the reason's capacity for totality or infinity should
> be invariably construed as power degrading the sensible and rescuing
> man from "humiliation" at the hands of nature. But though the sub-
> lime of magnitude does not originate in a power struggle, it almost

instantaneously turns into one as the secondary oedipal system takes over.[17]

If we step back a moment, it may now be possible to state, in a general and schematic fashion, just where the fascination of the mathematical sublime lies and what sort of problem it represents for the historian or the theorist. Weiskel's scrupulosity in raising the question of excess, in wishing not to suppress "a multitude of facts" in the interest of establishing a theoretical model, parallels Samuel Monk's qualm lest he impose a "false and artificial form" on a chaotic mass of material. We might even see in Weiskel's invocation of the (maternal) pre-oedipal phases, in his interpretation of them as constituting the deep (hence primary) structure of the sublime and yet as still only a tributary of the oedipal system, into which it invariably flows, a more serious and argued version of Monk's joking about the woman not fit to be seen. The goal in each case is the oedipal moment, that is, the goal is the sublime of conflict and structure. The scholar's *wish* is for the moment of blockage, when an indefinite and disarrayed sequence is resolved (at whatever sacrifice) into a one-to-one confrontation, when numerical excess can be converted into that supererogatory identification with the blocking agent that is the guarantor of the self's own integrity as an agent.

I suggested earlier that something similar could be seen at work during the eighteenth century, as the notion of difficulty or recalcitrance was transformed, through a passage to the limit, into the notion of absolute blockage. This, too, would seem to have been the result of a wish, for although the moment of blockage might have been rendered as one of utter self-loss, it was, even before its recuperation as sublime exaltation, a confirmation of the unitary status of the self. A passage to the limit may seem lurid, but it has its ethical and metaphysical uses.

STANDING FOR BLOCKAGE:
SCHOPENHAUER AND THE BLIND BEGGAR

At the beginning of this essay I proposed some paragraphs written by the scholar Thomas McFarland as a contemporary instance of the mathematical sublime. There, I suggested, we could trace a scenario that eighteenth-century theorists would have found familiar: the progress of the mind as it sought to take in a dismaying plurality of objects. If we look back at McFarland's text now, we should be able to bring its movement into clearer focus.

The mind is set in motion by a threat—the "exponential accumulation of secondary discussion," the "flood of publication"—but the threat is directed not at the exterior intellectual landscape (this is only a metaphorical "flood") but at the inner integrity of the mind itself, that is, at the integrity of the individual scholar's mind. No single reader can "claim to be competent to provide specialist commentary on more than a decade or two," McFarland notes. And it is the ideal of a cultured—i.e., broadly competent—individual that McFarland would defend. Hence, McFarland makes no attempt to "totalize" or "integrate" the objects of his dismay, whatever that might mean in practice (perhaps a reorganization of literary scholarship along more efficient lines?). Setting such activity aside as impracticable and no doubt undesirable in any case, and therefore checked in its commerce with its objects, the scholar's mind, in Kant's phrase, "sinks back into itself," not without, again in Kant's phrase, "a kind of emotional satisfaction": what is generated is a rhetoric of interior totalization, the plea for "the integration of awareness" and its embodiment in the figure of "man thinking." But at this point a further difficulty arises: for the scholar to contemplate the Emersonian description of "man thinking" is to be quite literally cast in the role of "man reading"; or, more accurately, to discern that one's thinking and one's reading are, in the best of scholarly times (and when would that have been? before what Fall?), hard to disentangle. It is in response to this puzzling recognition that the figure of Schopenhauer is called up. He appears as McFarland's double, reiterating his dismay, seconding his call for an integration of awareness in still more authoritative tones. But the presence of his words within quotation marks serves as one more reminder that "other people's ideas" are as much the material of genuine thinking as they are a hindrance to it. Schopenhauer, we could say, is the name of that difficulty; he stands for the recurrent and commonplace difficulty of distinguishing thinking from reading, and he is conjured up here as an agent of sublime blockage, an eloquent voice at the end of the line.[18]

But why this thrust toward eloquence and confrontation? My discussion of the eighteenth-century sublime suggests one answer: that the self cannot simply think but must read the confirmation of its own integrity, which is only legible in a specular structure, a structure in which the self can perform that "supererogatory identification with the blocking agent." That, I believe, is what drives McFarland to summon up Schopenhauer from the grave, and it is the same energy that erodes the stability of that specular poise: the voice of Schopenhauer gives way, to be replaced, in the next paragraph, by the fantasy of the computer. This grimly comic vision is set in the future ("The wheel will then have come full circle: computers will be writing for computers") but it is an embodiment of a threat that has been present all along. The computer is the machine inside the ghost of Schopenhauer, the system of energies that links "thinking" to "reading" to "remembering" to "citing" to "writing." It serves here as a figure for what makes scholars run, when that process is felt to be most threatening to the integrity of individual awareness, a threat from which even "the strongest are not free."

> Oh, blank confusion! true epitome
> Of what the mighty City is herself
> To thousands upon thousands of her sons,
> Living amid the same perpetual whirl
> Of trivial objects, melted and reduced
> To one identity, by differences
> That have no law, no meaning, and no end—
> Oppression, under which even highest minds
> Must labour, whence the strongest are not free.[19]

Bartholomew Fair, as it is imagined in the last lines of book 7 of *The Prelude*, was Wordsworth's computer, a city within the City, a scale model of urban mechanisms, designed to focus his fear:

> Tents and Booths
> Meanwhile, as if the whole were one vast mill,
> Are vomiting, receiving on all sides,
> Men, Women, three-years Children, Babes in arms.
>
> [718-21]

The lines on Bartholomew Fair repeat, in a condensed and phantasmagoric fashion, what had been the burden of the earlier accounts of London: the sometimes exhilarating, sometimes baffling proliferation, not merely of sights and sounds, objects and people, but of consciously chosen and exhibited modes of representation. Book 7 is the book of spectacle, theatricality, oratory, advertising, and *ad hoc* showmanship, not just the book of crowds. A Whitmanesque passage from early in the book catches the mixture as well as providing an instance of Wordsworth's own narrative—or rather, *non*narrative—stance:

> Rise up, thou monstrous ant-hill on the plain
> Of a too busy world! Before me flow,
> Thou endless stream of men and moving things!
> Thy every-day appearance, as it strikes—

With wonder heightened, or sublimed with awe—
On strangers, of all ages; the quick dance
Of colours, lights and forms; the deafening din;
The comers and the goers face to face,
Face after face; the string of dazzling wares,
Shop after shop, with symbols, blazoned names,
And all the tradesman's honours overhead:
Here, fronts of houses, like a title-page,
With letters huge inscribed from top to toe,
Stationed above the door, like guardian saints;
There, allegoric shapes, female or male,
Or physiognomies of real men,
Land-warriors, kings, or admirals of the sea,
Boyle, Shakespeare, Newton, or the attractive head
Of some quack-doctor, famous in his day.

[149-67]

These lines, so full of detail, are not exactly narrative; they
conjure more than they describe. And what they summon up
is a different order of experience from what we think of as
characteristically Wordsworthian. They resist the phenomenological reading that seems so appropriate elsewhere in *The Prelude*,
a reading attuned to the nuanced interinvolvements of centrally
Wordsworthian modes of experience—seeing and gazing, listening, remembering, feeling. Instead, they present a plethora of
prefabricated items—tradesmen's signs, statuary—that are
intended to be legible, not merely visible, and mix these in with
sights and sounds, "men and moving things," in rapid apposi-
tional sequence until everything comes to seem like reading
matter ("Face after face; the string of dazzling wares,/Shop
after shop, with symbols, blazoned names ... ").

As the book goes on, the prodigious energy Wordsworth
experiences in London is more and more made to seem a function of the tradesmen's and showmen's and actors' wish to
represent and of the populous's complementary hunger for
spectacle: representation comes to seem like the very pulse of
the machine. And in a startling moment, too strange to be

simply satirical, the showman's crude inventiveness and the audience's will to believe are brought into touch with the developing opposition between what can be seen and what can be read. Wordsworth is describing a performance of "Jack the Giant-killer" at Sadler's Wells:

> Lo!
> He dons his coat of darkness; on the stage
> Walks, and achieves his wonders, from the eye
> Of living Mortal covert, 'as the moon
> Hid in her vacant interlunar cave.'
> Delusion bold! and how can it be wrought?
> The garb he wears is black as death, the word
> 'Invisible' flames forth upon his chest.

> [280-87]

I have offered these citations and have been teasing out thematic strands as a way of suggesting the drift of book 7 toward a sublime encounter, the episode with the Blind Beggar, who occupies what we might call the "Schopenhauer position" in the structure of the poem. Wordsworth himself has been drifting through the book, sometimes presenting his experience anecdotally, in the autobiographical past tense ("I saw . . . ," "I viewed . . . ") that we are accustomed to in *The Prelude*, more often presenting himself as poet-impresario of the great spectacle, in a generalized present tense ("I glance but at a few conspicuous marks,/Leaving a thousand others, that, in hall,/ Court, theatre . . . "). Without forcing the poem, I think we can say that the difference between the subject of autobiographical experience and the poet-impresario is made to seem, in book 7 more than elsewhere in *The Prelude*, like the difference between seeing and reading. In London, more than in the country, everybody's experience is mediated by the semiotic intentions of others; in book 7, more than anywhere else in *The Prelude*, the poet adopts the showman's stance. I believe it is the developing confusion of these two roles, the odd slackening of the tension

between them, as much as the accumulating overload of urban
detail, that precipitates the critical scene with the Blind Beggar.
I cite the episode in its earlier version, which is less elegantly
worded but at one point more revealing:

> How often in the overflowing Streets,
> Have I gone forward with the Crowd, and said
> Unto myself, the face of every one
> That passes by me is a mystery.
> Thus have I look'd, nor ceas'd to look, oppress'd
> By thoughts of what, and whither, when and how,
> Until the shapes before my eyes became
> A second-sight procession, such as glides
> Over still mountains, or appears in dreams;
> And all the ballast of familiar life,
> The present, and the past; hope, fear; all stays,
> All laws of acting, thinking, speaking man
> Went from me, neither knowing me, nor known.

>   [1805 text, 594–606]

The last four lines of this passage, eliminated when Wordsworth revised the poem, tell of a moment, a recurrent moment,
of thoroughgoing self-loss—not the recuperable baffled self
associated with scenarios of blockage, but a more radical flux
and dispersion of the subject. The world is neither legible nor
visible in the familiar way: faces, which had earlier been associated with signs, are there but they cannot be deciphered, while
visible shapes have taken on a dreamlike lack of immediacy.
This loss of "ballast" is made to sound like the situation of
"blank confusion" at Bartholomew Fair, when objects become
"melted and reduced/To one identity, by differences/That
have no law, no meaning, and no end": it is not that differences
disappear, but that the possibility of interpreting them as significant differences vanishes. It may be, for instance, that seeing
and reading are not that distinct, that as the possibility of
interpreting differences diminishes, the possibility of distinguishing presentation from representation does too, and with it, the

possibility of drawing a clear demarcation between the subject
of autobiography and the poet-impresario. Some remarkable
effects can be generated by crossing that line (the famous
instance would be the rising-up of Imagination in book 6),
but the line needs to be established in order to be vividly trans-
gressed. These are the threats, this is the "ferment silent and
sublime" (8. 572), that inhere in these lines, and I believe it is
in response to them that the Blind Beggar is brought into the
poem:

> 'twas my chance
> Abruptly to be smitten with the view
> Of a blind Beggar, who, with upright face,
> Stood propp'd against a Wall, upon his Chest
> Wearing a written paper, to explain
> The story of the Man, and who he was.
> My mind did at this spectacle turn round
> As with the might of waters, and it seem'd
> To me that in this Label was a type,
> Or emblem, of the utmost that we know,
> Both of ourselves and of the universe;
> And, on the shape of the unmoving man,
> His fixèd face and sightless eyes, I look'd
> As if admonish'd from another world.

[1805 text, 609-22]

In one sense, the Beggar simply allows Wordsworth to reiterate
his sense of bafflement. Earlier he had told himself "the face of
every one/That passes by me is a mystery"; now he is faced
with an "emblem of the utmost we can know." And in the play
between the Beggar's blank face and the minimally informative
text on his chest, the difference between what Wordsworth
can see and what he can read is hardly reestablished in any
plenitude: it is a fixed difference—the text won't float up and
blur into the lineaments of the Beggar's face—but it is still
almost no difference at all. However, it is precisely the fixity
that is the point—a point that is softened in the direction of a

more intelligibly humane reading by Wordsworth's decision to change "His fixèd face" (1805) to "His steadfast face" (1850). The encounter with the Beggar triangulates the poet's self in relation to his double, who is represented, for a moment, as an emblem of minimal difference fixed in relation to itself. The power of the emblem is that it reestablished boundaries between representor and represented and, while minimizing the differences between them keeps the poet-impresario from tumbling into his text. I would suggest that this is the common function of the moment of blockage in sublime scenarios.

NOTES

1. Immanuel Kant, *Critique of Judgment*, trans. J. H. Bernard (New York: Hafner, 1966), p. 83.

2. Ibid., 91.

3. Thomas McFarland, "Recent Studies in the Nineteenth Century," *SEL* 16 (1976): 693–94.

4. William Wordsworth, *The Prose Works of William Wordsworth*, ed. W.J.B. Owen and Jane Worthington Smyser, 3 vols. (Oxford: Clarendon, 1975), 2: 355.

5. Samuel Monk, *The Sublime: A Study of Critical Theories in XVIII-Century England* (1935; reprint ed., Ann Arbor: University of Michigan Press, 1960), p. 58.

6. Ibid., p. 6.

7. Ibid., p. 3–4.

8. Thomas Weiskel, *The Romantic Sublime: Studies in the Structure and Psychology of Transcendence* (Baltimore: The Johns Hopkins University Press, 1976), pp. 22–33.

9. David Hume, *A Treatise of Human Nature*, ed. L. A. Selby-Bigge (Oxford: Clarendon, 1888), p. 436.

10. Angus Fletcher, *Allegory: The Theory of a Symbolic Mode* (Ithaca: Cornell University Press, 1964), pp. 234–35.

11. Alexander Gerard, *An Essay on Taste*, 2nd ed. (Edinburgh, 1764; reprinted, New York: Garland, 1970), p. 12.

12. Kant, *Critique of Judgment*, p. 91.

13. Weiskel, *Romantic Sublime*, p. 21.

14. Ibid., p. 41.

15. Ibid., pp. 92 ff.

16. Ibid., pp. 99 ff.

17. Ibid., p. 106.

18. This may be the moment to acknowledge some other people's ideas. Henry Abelove pointed out to me the nice irony, no doubt conscious on McFarland's part, of his selecting Schopenhauer for this particular role. Schopenhauer is the occasion for a peculiarly devious development in Proust's essay "On Reading." (Originally published as the preface to Proust's translation of Ruskin's *Sesame and Lilies* in 1906, the essay has been reprinted, in a bilingual edition, translated and edited by Jean Autret and William Burford [New York: Macmillan, 1971].) On p. 51, Proust offers Schopenhauer as "the image of a mind whose vitality bears lightly the most enormous reading"; on the next page, Schopenhauer is praised for having produced a book "which implies in an author, along with the most reading, the most originality"; between these two accolades Proust quotes a series of fifteen or so passages, taken, he says, from one page of *The World as Will and Representation*, which he strings together so as to produce a rapid, abbreviated, reiterative, and finally comical parade of bits of Voltaire, Byron, Herodotus, Heraclitus (in Latin), Theognis (in Latin), and so on, down to Byron (again) and Balthazar Gracian. The effect is like that of riffling the pages of Curtius; the whole run-through is punctuated by Proust's repetition of "etc." as he cuts off one citation after another. Josué Harari has drawn my attention to a fine reading of this essay by Barbara Harlow in *MLN* 90 (1975): 849-71.

19. William Wordsworth, *The Prelude*, ed. Ernest de Selincourt and Helen Darbishire (Oxford: Clarendon, 1959), p. 261. Henceforth, references to *The Prelude* will appear in the text; unless otherwise indicated, line numbers refer to the 1850 version of book 7.

Geoffrey H. Hartman

Psychoanalysis: The French Connection

1

> To be stripped of every fiction save one
> The fiction of an absolute
>
> Wallace Stevens

The language of Lacan and Derrida is shaped by a Heideggerian detour. Both writers see Western philosophy as reflecting through its grammar, its categories, and its now inbuilt manner of discourse a desire for reality-mastery as aggressive and fatal as Freud's death instinct. Their critique of metaphysics seems to blend with the findings of Freudian metapsychology. The Western thinker gloats over reality like Shakespeare's Achilles over the living body of Hector. Achilles, in a jocose and terrible taunt, inspects Hector as if he were infinitely vulnerable:

> Tell me you heav'ns, in which part of his body
> Shall I destroy him? whether there, or there,
> That I may give the local wound a name;
> And make distinct the very breach, whereout
> *Hector's* great spirit flew.
>
> [*Troilus and Cressida*, 4.9]

This fearful power of pointing out, or pointing at, expresses what Lacan describes as the phantasm of morcellation, or of the "corps morcelé"—a phantasm that the psyche is always seeking to allay. If we remember that Achilles is almost immortal, that in theory he can only be wounded through a heel left untouched by his immersion in the Styx, then we see the connection between this taunt and a deeply human anxiety. In ordinary mortals the Achilles heel is everywhere; psychic development is therefore a balance between the hope of immortality and the continuous fear of mortal exposure.

Directness—the "fingering" or "prenominating" mode of

Achilles—has its shadow side, which is part of the very subject of French investigations linking language and the psyche. Yet to say we are crucified, or morcellated, by language is as pathetic and exaggerated as to claim we are potentially redeemed by it. The fundamental concern of Lacan and Derrida is with directness, or *intellectual* passion: that rigorous striving for truth, exposure, mastery, self-identification—in short, science and metaphysics—which at once defines and ravages the human actor.

Against this rigor, and often from within it, various doctors including those of the Church have sought to defend us; poetry, too, has been considered a *remedium intellectus* and the poet-humanist a "physician to all men." It is not surprising, then, that Derrida should open his tortuous and capital work, *Glas*, with reflections on Hegel's "absolute knowledge"—that immediacy of person to truth which is the exact obverse of the naive immediacy Hegel calls "abstract" and which the absolute thinker sees filled or made concrete by historical experience in its very negativity, its morcellating if also self-healing movement.

Speaking of passion we evoke necessarily a family of words: "patience," "patient," "passio gloriosa," even "crime passionelle." In the column opposite to the one that opens with an allusion to Hegel's absolute thinker, Derrida quotes from Genet what seems to be a fit of passion or else a gratuitous act: the tearing to pieces of an essay manuscript on Rembrandt, rendered as if a picture itself, or the very name Rembrandt, had been defaced. "Ce qui est resté d'un Rembrandt déchiré en petits carrés réguliers et foutu aux chiottes" (*Glas*, 7b).* This strange onomatoclastic act is directed against what I will call "l'imago du nom propre" (the imago of the proper name) and it again evokes the fantasy of the "corps morcelé." We are made to realize how easily the psyche is punctured by image, photo,

*See Bibliographical Note at end of essay.

phantasm, or phrase. The terrible rigor of psychic, like logicistic, process sets this human vulnerability in a perversely radiant frame, one that may extend toward infinity like the Chinese torture of "a hundred pieces." Psychoanalysis, in this light, reveals once more the unresolvable ambivalence of passion as both suffering and ecstasy: as a *geometry* of beatitude achieved by submitting again and again to the wounding power of some ultimate penetration, or the illusion of coming "face to face" with life or death or truth or reality.

"I am half-sick of shadows," says Tennyson's Lady of Shallott, before she turns to what she thinks is reality and dies. The wish to put ourselves in an unmediated relation to whatever "really" is, to know something absolutely, means a desire to be defined totally: marked or named once and for all, fixed in or by a word, and so—paradoxically—made indifferent. "He (She) desired to be without desire" is the underlying clue in the psychodrama of many Lacanian patients. The story of I (for identity) begins to cheapen into the Story of O, and can be more dehumanizing even in the noble form of Descartes's "cogito ergo sum" than the dangers of the Id. Pornosophy, so at home in France, so alien to English and American literature, depicts prophylactically the Ego's demanding a "divine" violation into thinghood or invulnerability. The indeterminacy principle, however, that Lacan and Derrida develop from dream logic and literary language begins with the Id rather than with the Ego: or minimally with the *id est*, which, like the *à savoir* ("namely"), defers absolute knowledge and definitive naming in the very act of exemplary instancing. "Id est, ergo id non est." Exemplification is always serial, subversive, plural.

We return by this route to the subtle links between psyche and language. For one wonders, in reading Lacan, whether philosophical discussions concerning the *stigme*, or "here and now," are so removed, after all, from psychoanalytic speculations on the divine or hysterical stigmata, and the whole issue of ecstasy, identification, incorporation, conversion. Did Freud really succeed in ushering in an era of "deconversion" or of purely "psychological man"? With Lacan in particular, the project of psychoanalysis is not only involved in what the relation of analyst and analysand may mean for the "order of discourse" each embodies—just as Derrida, in *Glas*, explores simultaneously the question of a relation between the paternal discourse of a magister ludi called Hegel and the thievish, maternal "calculus" revealed by Genet. Lacan's project is not only this sensitive exploration of the power relations between codes or idioms within language; it is also an attempt to restructure them, in order to build a new communitarian model on the basis of psychiatric experience. Though we have entered the age of Freud we remain in the age of Saint-Simon.

Lacan exposes the self-protective devices and rules so important to Freudian psychiatry, and demands of the clinician that he listen to the "Other" who is as much in himself as in the patient. This Other solicits the labor of recognition that must keep analyst and analysand apart despite transference and countertransference. The "pathos" of the analytic situation is linked to its representational character: something is acted out here-and-now to cure the here-and-now by a respect for there-and-then; for difference, otherness, change, mortality. The patient is to become patient rather than fitful-passionate, and the analyst must be patient too in order to *hear* what is going on, to decipher or even redeem from the *res* the *rebus* presented to him. "Hieroglyphics of hysteria, blazons of phobia, labyrinths of the *Zwangsneurose*—charms of impotence, enigmas of inhibition, oracles of anxiety, talking arms of character, seals of self-punishment, disguises of perversion—these are the hermetic elements that our exegesis resolves, the equivocations that our invocation dissolves, the artifices that our dialectic absolves."

Yet the analyst is attracted to and therefore protects himself from the ecstatic message, the heart of darkness in the patient, that is, in himself. He hunts that wounded hart as in some spiritual chase, but only to build on it (strange rock that weeps) an acknowledgment of a purely human crucifixion, of a secular, self-inflicted stigmatics.

Freud, according to Lacan, founded psychoanalysis on this attraction to the hysterical patient, usually a woman; and inattention to that origin means that theory must "cherchez la femme" once again, or take "le discours de la femme" (the woman's word) again into the method. A quasisacred detective story unfolds as Lacan follows the traces, semiobliterated, of Freud. He begins his own career with a thesis of 1932 that reflects on what is practically a literary theme: the self-inflicted wound of a woman he calls Aimée. The question elaborated since 1932 is that of the "Eigentlichkeit" or "propriety" of this wound, one that is contagious in the sense that it cannot be localized, much less contained. Lacan's thesis is that the erotomanic woman who knifed an actress was really attacking her own person: the mystery is that the wound had to go through that detour.

In much of his work Lacan interprets a "blessure" (wound) that is so ambivalently a "blessing" as the *symptom* that acts out whatever is human in us. He names the wound, or makes "distinct the very breach" that renders the psyche visible. It is a movement of desire that cannot define itself except as a desire of, and belonging to, an other: a desire that may not be appropriated by the self, and so cannot build up (as ego psychology would have it) a stable self. In terms of sexual differentiation the breach is related to the (absent) phallus and in terms of noncarnal conversation it is related to a language where the signifier cannot be completed by the signified. The phallus as signifier is not circumscribed by its function of procreation but serves to open the wound, and womb, of signification. If the psyche is said to be structured like language it is because the symptom is always like a displaced or forgotten word, a repressed signifier that pretends to be *the* signified and a terminus to desire. The analyst recovers the signifier and with that not only the meaning of symptoms but a blocked mode or force of speech. Hence, all psychoanalysis draws others into its contagious orbit and stimulates an epidemic of soul-(un)making. The history of religion is full of such epidemics, of course; and Lacan's project, however self-aware, remains under that shadow.

I am consciously reading Lacan (and also Derrida) in the light of what Sartre called "la grande affaire"—the scandal of theological survivals in even the most secular thinkers. This survival may simply mean that the concept of secularization as presently understood is premature or crude. It is clear, however, that French thought in the area of psychoanalysis has removed language from the hope of being purified through a curative metalanguage. A language that is authentic, that lies beyond the eloquence of wounds or religious pathos or the desire for reality-mastery, is not to be found. Lacan, in this, must sometimes be distinguished from his followers, whose belief in the truth of words is more directly thaumaturgic and whose case histories can be more transparent and frightening in their reductionist clarity than those of the early Freud. At best both Lacan and Derrida remind us that language, like sexual difference or passion in general, is that in which we live and breathe and have our being. It cannot be subdued but remains part of the subtle knot that perplexes even as it binds together man and woman in the "scène familiale."

2

Que tu brilles enfin, terme pur de ma course
Valéry, "Fragments du Narcisse"

In a glass darkly. Lacan discovers a "stade du miroir" (mirror phase) in the early development of what is to be the child's ego. By the complaisance of the mirror the child sees itself for the first time as a coordinated being, and triumphantly, jubilantly, assumes that image. But what is found by means of this play ("je-jeu") with the mirror is really a double rather than a differentiated other. The myth of Narcissus is given clinical verisimilitude. The other (Rimbaud: "Je est un autre") is necessary for self-definition, but in the mirror is simply an illusory unification. The "corps morcelé," moreover, the fragmented or uncoordinated body image prior to the mirror phase, is only suspended. It remains active in the domain that Lacan names the verbal or symbolic in contrast to the nonverbal or imaginary.

Beyond these observations lies a difficult psychopathology that we need not oversimplify except to say that the concept of a "corps morcelé" (cf. *Glas*, "un Rembrandt déchiré") is connected with Lacan's understanding of the castration complex, or how the phallus or the body part that "represents" the sexual foundation of otherness is enmeshed in an extraordinary developmental series of differential yet substitutive (compensatory) mechanisms. Acceptance of the (absent) phallus, or of the (absent) father, or, basically, of the mediacy of words, allows a genuine recognition of difference.

Since the mirror phase, although using gestaltist and biological evidence, is not securely based on experimental data (especially when compared to the painstaking work of Piaget) it might be better to call it the *Marienbad complex*. Not only is Marienbad where the hypothesis was first made public, but also Resnais's film, *Last Year at Marienbad*, expresses Lacan's mirror domain as a fact of the imagination: the image or heroine in that film's mobile mirror seems to quest for a specular yet totally elusive identity, for some unique reduction to one place, one time, one bed, one fixative spectral event.

The mirror phase, then, deals with images, with thing rather than word representation. (In the *Marienbad* film, the sound track is dissociated from the life of the images, running nonparallel with it, an arbitrary or contrapuntal yet related experience. It is exactly like the somewhat mysterious juxtaposition, in Lacan, of symbolic and imaginary spheres.) The notion of a "corps morcelé" does, however, connect with the differential system of a psycholinguistics. The question therefore arises: is there anything comparable to the mirror stage on the level of language?

Lacan's emphasis on the birth of language out of a "symbolic" rather than "imaginary" sphere seems to moot this line of inquiry. He suggests that the specular image, as the base of other imagery that serves an integrative or unifying function, is an illusory modification of a deeper or prior system, inherently differential. Thus, the question of what corresponds to the mirror phase on the level of language (to its unifying if illusory effect) may seem unanswerable in terms of Lacanian psychiatry.

Yet there is the well-known magical or religious ambition to possess *the* word. Does not the concept of Word or Logos in religion, or in such artists as Hölderlin, provide a clue? And is not the Lacanian psychopompos, who recovers an interior signifier, of that tradition? We are looking for a correlative in language to the specular image. The logos understood as that in whose "image" whatever is is signifying seems to motivate a logocentric phase of development—the very thing Derrida is seeking to expose.

Or consider the importance of the proper name in Shakespeare. "Had I it written, I would tear the word," Romeo says to Juliet, referring to his family name. The wounding of a name is too much like the wounding of the body not to be significant. We don't know why Genet tore "Rembrandt," but the effacing or defacing of the proper name suggests that there may be such a thing as a specular name or "imago du nom propre" in the fantasy development of the individual, a name more genuinely one's own than a signature or proper name. Signatures can always be faked. Is there something that cannot be faked? "The signature is a wound, and there is no other origin to the work of art" (*Glas*, 207). Is it possible to discern a specular word, logos phase, or imago of the proper name in the development of the individual?

Derrida's reflections on Hegel, in *Glas*, open with a play on the idea of "naming" or "nomination," a theme fully elaborated in his juxtaposed column on Genet. He implies, without calling it so, an imago of the proper name on the basis of what we know of the haunting, fixative, unifying effect of "being named." Just as the specular image produces a jubilant awareness tested and affirmed by the child's mirror mimicry, so the specular name can produce a hallelujah and magnifying language that mimics a sublimity associated with the divine logos. This is so even if the identifying name, the "nom unique" or "nom propre," is accusatory. Indeed the *scene of nomination* (my own phrase) is bound to be "accusative" as well as "nominative," or to include within it a reflexive, intense response to the act of vocative designation. "You are a thief," that commonplace accusation, that merest insult addressed to Genet as a child, strikes inward as a divine apostrophe and perhaps founds the perverse, high ritualism of his style.

In such a scene of nomination, then, the mirror speaks. We suspect, of course, that our primary narcissism has already spoken to it, like the queen in *Snow White*. But whatever question has been put remains obscure: only the mirror's response is clear, indeed so clear that it obliges us to assume its answer as an identity, to construct or reconstruct some feature in us clarified by this defining response. At the same time, the specular name or identity phrase—our true rather than merely proper name—is reaffirmed *in time* by a textual mimicry, joyful, parodistic, or derisory, of the original "magnification." The repetition of the specular name gives rise to texts that seem to be anagrammatic or to conceal an unknown-unknowable key, a "pure" signifier. These texts are called literature.

Can we assert that the specular name "exists"? Derrida knows that such words as "exist" and "is" point to a static order of things and he tries to avoid the trap of this inbuilt language-metaphysic. He suggests, instead, that if there is a Hegelian *Sa* (*savoir absolu*) it may be incompatible with the *Sa* (*signifiant*) we call a signature: the proper name (Hegel) affixed to a text as its authenticating seal.

A similar counterpointing of proper and specular name is suggested in Genet's case. The "antherection" of his name in a given passage (that is, the flowry style that alludes to his flower name, "genêt") makes a tomb of it: as in Saussure's anagrams, the text generated by the name is bound to enlace and so to bury it. Like a child who will not believe his parents are his real parents but engages imaginatively in a "family romance," so the proper name, or signature, is always being "torn up" in favor of a specular name, whether or not it can be found:

> The grand stakes of discourse (I mean *discourse*) that is literary: the patient, tricky, quasi animalistic or vegetative transformation, unwearying, monumental, derisive also, but turning derision rather against itself—the transformation of the proper name, *rebus*, into things, into the name of things. (*Glas*, 11a)

More radically still: writing is coterminous with that canceling movement, "la nécessité du passage par la détermination biffée, la nécessité de ce *tour d'écriture*." Every return, then, as in Genet, to a scene of nomination, must be unmasked as a figure. It introduces a factitious present or fictitious point of origin that may not be taken literally ("livré à la police") unless we are in search of an "ordinateur secret" leading back to baptism or birth. "A text only exists, resists, consists, represses, lets itself be read or written if it is elaborated [*travaillé*] by the unreadability [*illisibilité*] of a proper name. I have not said—not yet—that such a proper name exists and that it becomes unreadable when it falls [or is entombed, *tombe*] into the signature. The proper name does not ring forth [*résonne*], lost at once, save at the instant of its *débris*, when it breaks—embroils—

checks itself on touching the signature [*seing*]" (*Glas*, 41b).

Glas ends, therefore, with the words "le débris de" [Derrida] —that is, it touches, without actually stating, the "seing." The proper name seems to have been "disseminated": *Glas* has told (tolled) its demise. This concept of dissemination moves to the fore in Derrida's writings after the *Grammatology*. It is essential for his critique of Lacan or Sartre or any hermeneutic that relapses into a thematics (even a polythematics) by its insistence on an explanatory "key." In his grimly funny way, Derrida compares this procedure of "slipping the universal passkey into all lacunae of signification" to a police action. "It would mean arresting once again, in the name of the law, of veracity, of the symbolic order, the free movement [*marche*] of an unknown person" (*Glas*, 36b).

The signature, which denotes propriety through the proper name, is the *cas limite* of this arrest. Only courts of justice should insist on it, with their cumbersome machinery of registration, verification, ceremonial gravity, etc. Dissemination is, strangely enough, a pastoral though totally uninnocent protest against such restrictive or paralegal types of hermeneutic. It is the obverse, in fact, of classification. "What makes us write is also what scatters the semes, disperses *signacoupure* and *signacouture*" (*Glas*, 192b).

The passage from cl (for "class," "clé," "clue") to gl (for "glas" or "glu") analogizes these contraries: classification and dissemination. "At the very moment," Derrida continues, "we try to seize, in a particular text, the workings of an idiom, linked to a chain of proper nouns and actual denotative configurations, *glas* also names *classification*, that is, their inscription in networks of generalities infinitely articulated, or in the genealogies of a structure whose crossweaving, coupling, switching, detouring, branching can never be derived merely from a semantic or a formal rule. There is no absolute idiom or signature. . . . The bell tolls always for the idiom or the signature.

For the absolute precursor" [*aieul absolu*: perhaps "primal father"] (*Glas*, 169b).

Thus, we enter a chain of secondary elaborations stretching to infinity. There is no way of tracing them to an origin, to a logos that may have been "In the Beginning." When, in a quasiheraldic moment—talking arms of character, Lacan might say—Nerval's *Desdichado* recites, "Je suis le ténébreux, le veuf, l'inconsolé," we know that the family name "Labrunie" has been cast out in favor of a specular identity that is the widowed logos itself: the babel of "à la tour abolie." The appropriate hermeneutic, therefore, is like the interminable work of mourning, like an endless affectional detachment from the identity theme as such, whether that is linked to the (absent) logos or to a maternal and sexual presence distanced by the logos into the idea of an Immaculate Conception.

Perhaps the most persistent—obsessive—theme in *Glas* is the Immaculate Conception. It surges into the opening page before its time. No sooner has the author said, in the margin, "*Sa* will henceforth be the mark [*sigle*] of absolute knowledge," than he ads, "And *IC*, let us note it already, because the two portals [i.e., columns on the page] represent each other mutually, the mark of the Immaculate Conception." The notion of *sigle* (of words represented by their first letter) enters a series including "signature" and "seing" (seal or mark at the end of a text, representing the signatory, with a possible interlingual pun on *seing/sein/Sein*: seal/breast/Being). This tripling could be explained by the special function assigned each term but Derrida is more concerned with how language moves by marginal differentiation through a signifying series that can never quite circumscribe, or comprise, a body (corpus).

This term *Sa*, therefore, which he institutes but which is homophonic with Saussure's abbreviation for signifier (*signifiant*), although made of first and last (of *initial* letters that denote an *end* state) is neither a first or last term, for it enters an indefinite sequence that includes other words already mentioned, as well as *signe, ensigner, enseigner*, etc. Writing *Glas* in two columns, or beginning with two Hegel passages, reinforces our awareness that the "scene of writing" never takes place in one place: its locus (corpus) is always also "ein anderer Schauplatz," as Freud put it: displaced from right to left, to a supplementary comment or even into a physical symptom, which Lacan rightly analogizes to a "truth" already written down elsewhere and therefore in part missing from present discourse. There is, in short, no absolute or transcendental *Sa* (signifier) any more than an absolute or certain *Sa* (knowledge of what is signified). We cannot say, like Christ, "This is my body" without being already dead: premonumentalized.

From the start of *Glas*, then, we are presented with two illusory moments of ecstatic identification some 1800 years apart. They are (1) absolute knowledge, or Hegel's vision of an end to dialectic and alienation in the thought process of the philosopher who has internalized history; and (2) the phantasm of the Immaculate Conception. Why the latter? What bearing has it, as developed in the column on Genet, on the Hegelian "legend" unfolded opposite? And why emphasize, of all literary writers, Genet? Among Anglo-American readers the juxtaposition will cause a resistance which even the brilliance of the result may not remove.

These questions I will now try to explore a bit further. One must acknowledge, however, the problem of cultural difference that stands in the way. The pressure Derrida exerts on texts is admirable: through him we realize once more how consistently the human condition is a verbal condition. But there is little in English letters to compare with the *involution* of French or German commentary once it has singled out its exempla. A modern medievalism then takes over. So that, while the intertextual method opens its chosen books to endless interpretation, it also, paradoxically, affects the English or American reader as culturebound. The allusiveness goes inward rather than abroad, and we must start with the fact that Derrida's analysis of Genet is underwritten by a prior analysis, by local canon making or even canonization ("Saint Genet") that obliges him to meet that other Hegelian, Sartre, on common ground.

3

For there is a language of flowers.
For there is a sound reasoning upon all flowers.
C. Smart, Jubilate Agno

Sartre saw in Genet a "choix originel" or "projet existentiel" (*Glas*, 36b) maintained for thirty years and transformed into an occult religion and system of life. Like Lacan in psychiatry, Sartre posits, according to Derrida, a "transcendental key" that might open every text or psyche, slipping "into all signifying lacunae" like a "universal phallus." But if such a key exists, adds Derrida, it is already inscribed in Genet's own text as the "verge d'acier" or "bite ailée" he calls his pen. "I was haunted by it," writes Genet. "I slept beside it because a warrior sleeps armed."

So that if there is a key, the author has locked the text and, as it were, thrown the key away—into the text. This view seems to invert Lacan's understanding of psychosis, in which the key—the "nom-du-père"—is foreclosed by being "verworfen" or expelled (through hallucination) from the symbolic order into reality. Derrida also operates another reversal on Lacan. Genet's "verge d'acier" or "steel rod"—the pen-phallus—is said to belong less to the father than to the mother: to the mother as the Virgin. The pen-penis is like a "nom-de-plume" that represents the "nom-de-mère" instead of the "nom-du-père," or what *Glas* calls "le calcul de la mère."

Derrida's interest is chiefly in this phantom mother, or her discourse, which he prefers to call a *calcul* because it is at once complex and mute. The only words we have are Genet's own, and perhaps the fact so determining in Sartre's eyes, that Genet as a boy was accused of being a thief and took his identity from that. Derrida agrees that the insult, literalized, allowed the child to give himself back to his "true" mother, to identify with what is really *her* condition, that of having to draw an identity out of being abandoned. Abandoned in the absolute sense: *verworfen* or *geworfen*, without husband, father, father in heaven.

Derrida projects her image as a person without "Eigentlichkeit" and therefore also without a sense (and certainly not a bourgeois sense) of "Eigenschaften" or properties: "The mother is a thief and a beggar. She appropriates everything because she has nothing that is her own [*en propre*]" (170b). He makes her, wittily, a Heideggerian "Thing," even a "Ding-an-Sich." This vastated being, however, is not filled with grace, like the Virgin, but with ersatz; she is immaculate because she can't be stained by any gift, wound, or word. These are mere fillers of her non-essence, decorative substitutes, votive nothings. Like certain phantoms she has the capacity of incorporating all the names, abusive or exalted, magnifying or mourning, her son bestows until she becomes, in this double function of identity-vamp and muse, what is called untranslatably, a "bourreau berceur."

Not only, then, is Genet's work nourished by "poisoned milk," but it is drawn ineluctably to a fantasy that transforms the Christ legend more radically than Yeats's "Crazy Jane" poems. The mother is seen as Mary's double, just as Mary had such a double, Mary Magdalen, who "was able to engage on an infinite change of phallus without being changed [*detaillé*: literally, divided up or retailed]," the ultimate phallus involving her acceptance of Christ (*Glas*, 290b).

Even Genet's pen-phallus has a special relevance to the Christ legend. The lilies offered to the Virgin in pictures of the Annunciation are associated with the flower theme (*anthème*) of

Genet's style ("style" being itself, since Derrida never misses a trick, a flower term) that makes his book (*lit*, a reading) into a bed (*lit*) of flowers resembling a floral tomb. The pen-phallus or "verge [vierge] d'acier" reappears as the gladiolus, a name that means a little sword; in German "sword-lily." "Through my very soul," Mary says, "A sword shall pass, this is my favor'd lot/My exaltation to afflictions high" (Milton, *Paradise Regained* 2.90-92; Luke 2.34-5). Thus all of Genet's flowers of speech are at once pure and guilty (*coupable*), like the phantom mother. His own name is the proof of this strange purity: it derives from the plant called "genet" (ginestra, broom), which was his mother's, not his father's, name. He is a flower-child, then, even a virgin's child, however *coupable* as a thief, homosexual, and phallic being.

We understand better now the two-column structure of *Glas*. "Hegel and the discourse of the father" is matched by "Genet and the discourse (calcul) of the mother." Derrida not only brings out the "family romance" in Hegel's thought but suggests that what Hegel leaves behind in the march of the dialectic toward absolute knowledge is precisely the "du reste" from which Genet seems to build the dark purity of his work. According to Derrida we cannot reduce the coexistence of innocence and culpability in Genet's "language of flowers"—identified through Mallarmé with literariness itself—and whose ambivalence is exactly as Freud described it at two points in *The Interpretation of Dreams*. Yet Derrida is not concerned with setting Freud or Genet against Hegel and exposing the ambivalence of such symbols. He is formulating a hermeneutics of indeterminacy.

In Freud the underside of symbols is necessarily sexual, even when sexuality is not what is important. Freud does not reduce dreams to sexual messages but insists rather that infantile sexual experience structures what is dreamed. Yet, for Derrida, if the phallus is always "winged," "plumy" or "disseminated," then it cannot be used in the manner of a key to lock or unlock a subject: that is, fix a person's truth or identity-theme, or found it in a drive like the libido. There is no more a Freudian than a Cartesian cognito: you cannot hypostatize a word-wound as the eloquent trauma that determines all. Even in France psycho-analysis remains, according to Derrida, logocentric: a displaced religious or metaphysical discourse in search of the logos or "nom unique," of a single defining wound for which life, or else death, is the cure.

4

Every literary narrative contains another narrative: however continuous or full the one seems to be, the other is discontinuous and lacunary. Jean-Luc Nancy has called this "other" narrative the "discours de la syncope." Given that our minds tend to overestimate, even when wary or ashamed of it, fictional writing, the reader is usually forced into the position of having to recover the "discours de la syncope," that is, the precariousness of all transitions, or the undecidability of fiction's truth. Every story is like Isabel's in Melville's novel *Pierre,* and every authoritative title or naming should be treated on the analogy of "Pierre, or the Ambiguities."

Yet this deepening sense of an endless or ungrounded or non-continuous discourse is not purely cautionary or destructive. There is something we can take away with us: a perception similar to that offered by myths and positive interpretation. Our vision of the psyche's vulnerability broadens and intensifies; it extends into the bowels of language, from images to names and to the pathos that insistently attends the giving or calling out of a name. However different the Gothic gloom of Melville's *Pierre* and Faulkner's *Absalom, Absalom,* both novels turn on the seductive centrality of a scene of recognition—of naming and acknowledgment. The concepts of vocation, initiation, and identity run parallel yet subordinate to that central hinge that Aristotle in the *Poetics* already discerned as essential to Greek tragedy.

The desire for a "here and now," fixed image or defining word, mystic portrait or identity-imposing story, is not dissociable, according to psychiatry, from family romance: the recognition scene is always a displaced or sublimated family scene. It is no different with the Christian scandal of the "Presence of the Word" (*logos spermatikos*) in the Immaculate Conception, or more precisely, in the Annunciation. Let me, therefore, recenter these reflections on the most famous scene of nomination in our culture: the Annunciation.

There are, of course, other scenes that show the word of God coming to earth with vocational force. But this episode is particularly relevant to Genet because it "magnifies" a woman; indeed, Mary's hymn, called the Magnificat after its Latin version, and recorded in Luke, has become part of Christian liturgy. Not only is the Presence of the Word in this scene of nomination also the Word of the Presence ("Hail, O favored one, the Lord is with you," Luke 1:28), but the transcendental signifier, as we might truly call it, issues in a Magnificat because it takes away a curse: of infertility, and more generally, in reference to woman, of impure, because infertile, menstruation. Mary's condition, moreover, could have shamed her (Matthew 1:18-20, Luke 1:24), but through the intervention of the angelic word a potential denunciation becomes an annunciation.

In Genet, profanely, the same structure holds. Denunciation is converted to Annunciation; the curse (perhaps that of being born of woman, or male seed considered as impure, as a menstrual flow, *unless* made fertile in the woman) is taken away; and the Magnificat of a convict's style results. How "you are a thief" should become functionally equivalent to the sanctifying "you are with child" is the psychic puzzle that Sartre and Derrida try to resolve.

It is not by chance that Derrida should choose to continue through Genet his critique of the "closure" imposed on thought or language by the so-called logocentric tradition. Within that closure even miracles have their limits: virgin birth, or fulness (of grace) must be female. A male parthenogenesis is "inconceivable," even as miracle, except through the ultimate veil of theologic mystery. Scenes of nomination that affect men in scripture tend in fact, as with Abraham, to be a call for child sacrifice. But Freudian pornosophy has the bad taste to raise the question of whether the artist's work is not a male childbirth, and his book a "proles sine matre nata" (Montesquieu).

"You are a thief" can only stand for "you are with child" if, at some level, Genet is trying to steal the womb itself—whereas he can at most, if we trust Ferenzci's bioanalysis, steal *into* the womb and give something to that death in order to live. Genet is not successful in modifying even imaginatively the logocentric enclosure: he simply erects a subversive, symmetrical counterpart, the image of male fulness of grace, "L'annonce fait à Jean-Marie." Sound reasoning on his flowery or anthographic style must include the thought that flowers such as the lilies of the field or those associated with the Annunciation are pure in the sense that Hegel caught when he posits a nonagonistic "religion of flowers": they can grow and multiply as if by grace, without the curse of labor (cf. Genesis 3:16 ff.). The commandment, by place the first in the Bible, "Be fruitful and multiply," is death to hear, as Adams remarks in Milton's *Paradise Lost* (10.731), for it means, after the Fall, a multiplying of deaths or, as for Genet, *genitality with no grace except as it "blesses" a woman.* His family of thieves and murderers is erected in vain opposition to the survival of the "onto-theologic" model in secular society.

Genet's mirror image of the Holy Family, then, expresses a reversal rather than a transvaluation of values. Given the conservative character of the institution of language, it is doubtful that there could be transvaluation. We can reverse or trope catachresically, we can deploy all the subversive flowers in the anthology of speech, or we can reverse in another sense, by deconstruction, and expose the fallacy that every great artist's mind passes on itself—the result remains a secret recognition scene. As Genet himself has written: "The world is turned inside out like a glove. It happens that I am the glove and I understand at last that on the day of judgment God will call me with my own voice: 'Jean, Jean'" (*Glas*, 220b). Or Lacan: "The Word always subjectively includes its own reply. . . . The function of Language is not to inform but to evoke. What I seek in the Word is the response of the other. . . . In order to find him, I call him by a name which he must assume or refuse in order to reply to me." "The allocution of the subject entails an allocutor . . . even if he is speaking 'off' or 'to the wings.' He addresses himself to *ce (grand) Autre* whose theoretical basis I have consolidated. . . . "

Even the most deliberate counterannunciation yet conceived, Mallarmé's mirror scene in the *Herodiade*, can only use the language of flowers against itself. "Vous mentez, o fleur nue de mes lèvres." Herodiade's specular cries know they have no issue. Devoted to sterility, Herodiade is Mary's opposite in the drama of the logos that eventuates so curiously in Genet's (or Derrida's) image of the mother as "bourreau berceur." The logos as the *relève* (*Aufhebung*/fulfilment) of metaphor reifies metaphor and suppresses language fertility. Christ and Herod become co-conspirators in this Genet-ic massacre.

5

"Vous mentez," that denunciation so often addressed to the artist, is now, in the Nietzsche-(Wilde)-Derrida line of thinking, the only annunciation. It is addressed to language itself, "fleur nue de nos lèvres." Lacan, following Heidegger, is tempted to

ground language, or the symbolic realm, in that peculiar men-
dacity, or error, or untruth. The second part of *Being and Time*
(especially paragraphs 54–60) contains an analysis of the
elusiveness of the quest for truth in terms of self-identity. Such
a quest is based on a *Sich-Verhören*, a word that in German
denotes at one and the same time our attempt to know the
truth by taking the self into custody and interrogating it, and
the failure of that attempt, since a mishearing or mistaking of
what has been said is inevitable. Language gives the lie to the
ego's capture of a specular identity just as it gives the lie to
itself. The genuine logos is always a dia-logos; and the guardian
spirit of the symbolic and differential realm is a Father barring
the image's closure of dialogue, of stilling prematurely what one
might call, after Hegel, the *elaboration* of the negative.

Yet to ground something in untruth is still to ground it. Is a
true untruth better than an untrue truth? The dialectics become
dizzying or Ibsenian. Truth (*vérité*) remains, moreover, an important word for Lacan, and Derrida objects to it, as Adorno to
a Heidegger-influenced "jargon of authenticity." It might also
be observed that the symbolic father (or Derrida's counterpart,
the spectral mother), while a reformulation of Freud's dead
primal father of *Totem and Taboo*, has no more clinical or veri-
fiable reality than the "fair Lady of Shallot" in Tennyson's
poem of that name, who seems to be both victim and guardian
of the specular capture Lacan posits. This allusion shows, however, that a *sort* of evidence exists, even if contaminated by the
very realm—literature or art—being limited by scientific definition.

Derrida is very aware of this contamination, which he decon-
structs rather than denies or delimits. He does not place language,
by theoretical fiat, on the side of the symbolic and against the
specular realm of the absolute or totalizing illusion. Language
is not a "cause" that cures (a "talking cure") by drawing the
mirror image into the discourse of the Other. Though Derrida

views language as a School of Virtue chastening the eternally narcissistic ego, he sees no triumph of the therapeutic by means of a language that is itself infected by a sickness unto death he has labeled logo-centrism.

"I am half-sick of shadows," says the Lady of Shallot, and turns from her mirror to the reality of advent. She did not know that by her avertedness, by staying within representation, she had postponed death. The most art can do, as a mirror of language, is to burn through, in its cold way, the desire for self-definition, fulness of grace, presence; simply to expose the desire to own one's own name, to inhabit it numinously in the form of "proper" noun, words, or the signatory act each poem aspires to be. Though Tennyson's Lady, unlike Mallarmé's Herodiade, "knows not what the curse may be" as she helps to weave Tennyson's language, the result is the same: a negative scene of nomination. She becomes in death what she was without knowing it in life: a floating signifier.

> Under tower and balcony,
> By garden-wall and gallery,
> A gleaming shape she floated by,
> Dead-pale between the houses high,
> Silent into Camelot.
> Out upon the wharfs they came,
> Knight and burgher, lord and dame,
> And round the prow they read her name,
> *The Lady of Shalott.*

My reference to Tennyson suggests that a *sortie* from the textual involution of the French sphere is possible. Derrida has himself tried interpreting Poe, who is comparable to Tennyson, yet does not provide a true exit because French commentary has been investing him since Baudelaire and Mallarmé. The trouble with Tennyson is that his poetic dream-work seems at first no work at all. It is so easy, so unlabored—deceptively "idle," to use a charged word of his own—when held beside

Mallarmé's. Poem and lady remain immaculate though web, mirror, or spell may break. Such impassibility is perhaps part of the infection, an unresolved narcissism of festering lily or psyche. Yet this liaison between specular and poetic is precisely what fosters the illusion of completeness and so the attractive fetish we call a poem. For a moment the et cetera of language is absorbed into that fetish: remnant and rhyme coincide.

Derrida, however, does not allow himself even so much dallying with closure. The rhyming properties of language, the sonic rings and resonances always potentially there, are like Poe's "The Bells" (cited by him) and their telltale symptoms of a vertiginous *glissement* of language toward an uncontrollable echoing: a mad round of verbal associations or signifier-signifying signifiers. The anxiety roused by language *as* language is that this echoing movement cannot be economized, that it is a fluid curse, a telling that is merely that of time, whose wasting becomes a tolling: *Glas.*

6

His adventure is
having been *named.*

Sartre, *Saint Genet*

. . . the difficulty begins with the name.
Ralph Waldo Ellison, "Hidden Name and Complex Fate"

The subject too, if he can appear to be
the slave of language, is all the more
so of a discourse in the universal
movement, in which his place is
already inscribed at birth, if only
by virtue of his proper name.
Lacan, "The Agency of the Letter in
the Unconscious or Reason since Freud"

My hypothesis, inspired by French reflections, that literature is the elaboration of a specular name, is not meant to encourage a new substantialism of the word. Since the specular name is always already a fiction—hidden or forgotten or canceled, or motivated unconsciously by a life that dies into allegory—it can determine autobiographical quests only in the manner of Plato's theory of anamnesis. The quest, as it becomes lifelong and remains indeterminate, recuperates esoteric traditions: stories about the magic of names, anagrammatic events of various kinds, scenes of nomination or annunciation, and generally, to steal the title of Karl Abraham's early essay, "the determining force of names."

Gershom Scholem has published a strange name fantasy of Walter Benjamin's, written at Ibiza, Spain, in 1933. I would like to conclude with it. It involves Paul Klee's picture *Angelus Novus* (a personal icon for Benjamin, who owned it) and the ancient tradition of the natal genius or personal angel whose name is hidden but who represents one's true identity and secret self. Benjamin's allegory, close in some respects to a Kafka parable and in other respects to a Baudelaire prose poem, was deeply linked to his situation at that time: his troubled relation to women, his Jewish ancestry, and his sense of being born under Saturn (he had written *The Origin of German Tragedy* and was steeped in Baudelaire). Scholem's beautiful and thorough interpretation has brought this out in a definitive way, and I cannot add to what he has said.

My interest lies elsewhere; in Benjamin's fantasy as a particularly revealing example of how autobiography is determined by the idea of a hidden—spectral or specular—name. I will quote only the opening paragraphs, which constitute about half of this interesting document, but they suffice to show how Benjamin verges on a complex scene of nomination: an angelus-annunciation that turns not only on the magical force of an occult name but also on what might happen when that name is or must be betrayed.

Agesilaus Santander

When I was born the thought came to my parents that I might perhaps become a writer. Would it not be good, then, if not everybody
noticed immediately that I was a Jew. That is why they gave me in
addition to the name by which I was called [*Rufnamen*] two further,
exceptional ones, from which it couldn't be perceived either that a Jew
bore them or that they belonged to him as first names [*Vornamen*].
Forty years ago no parents could have proved more far-seeing. What
they considered a remote possibility has come true. Except that the
precautions by which they meant to counter fate were set aside by the
one most concerned. That is to say, instead of making it public together
with his writings, he treated it as the Jews the additional name of their
children which remains secret. Indeed, they only communicate it to
them when they reach manhood. Since, however, this manhood can
occur more than once in a lifetime, and the secret name may remain the
same and untransfigured only for the pious, so to whoever is not pious
the change of name might be revealed all at once, with the onset of a
new manhood. Thus with me. But it remains the name, nevertheless,
which binds together the vital forces in strictest union, and which
must be guarded against the unauthorized [*Unberufenen*].

Yet this name is not at all an enrichment of the one it names. On the
contrary, much falls away from his image when that name becomes
audible. His image loses above all the gift of appearing to be human. In
the room I occupied in Berlin, before he stepped—armed and encased—
out of my name into the light, he fixed his picture on the wall: New
Angel. The Kabbala relates that in every instant [*Nu*] God creates a
numberless number of new angels, all of whom are only destined,
before they dissolve into nothing, to sing for a single moment the praise
of God before His throne. Such an angel the New one pretended to be
before he would name himself.

What emerges with startling clarity is the *aura* of being named
or imaged. Benjamin also said: "Things made of glass have no
'aura'" ("Die Dinge aus Glas haben keine 'Aura'"). So the
world he projects in his Romance of Being Named resists trans-
lucence or glassification: the very word "Agesilaus" strikes one
as the opposite of the word "Glas"—it contains g-l-a-s, in fact,
and becomes, as it were, its antonym. Recalling Benjamin's

interest in anagrams Scholem suggests that the title of his fantasy should be deciphered as "Der Angelus Satanas" (The Angel Satan), and he links it to the "New Angel" of Klee's picture that continued to haunt Benjamin. (See, especially, the ninth of his "Theses on the Philosophy of History," written not long before his death.) But one should add that the insistence of this picture in the writer's life is itself "demonic": it reveals a specular fixation on Benjamin's part, and seems to be transposed from German Romantic fiction or the gothic novella. However we unriddle it, "Agesilaus Santander" remains an abracadabra phrase that aims at reviving the aura of names, or of a naming with ritual and fixative power.

I doubt, then, that this title is decipherable in a single way. The difference in sound shape, for example, between Agesilaus and Angelus (Novus) could foreground the syllable "laus," to remind us of the Latin word for praise; if so, a relation might suggest itself between "Age"/"Ange" plus "laus" and the Kabbalistic angel whose essence is to praise God a single moment, an "Augen"-blick.

Other decipherings may be possible, but I will try only one more. Benjamin thinks of himself as a refugee: he has abandoned the orthodoxy of his fathers; he is in Spain, from which the Jews were expelled and a former home of the Kabbalists, whose mystical reflections on names was known to him through Scholem; the Nazis have come to power; and he ponders angels whose essence is not permanence but transience, whose newness is their nowness, or their flight from *Nu* to *Nichts*, as they praise and wait to be dissolved. Considering, then, that this scholar was doomed to wander, if not to flee, and that his major work had been on seventeenth-century German literature, might he not have remembered the poet of that era who took the pseudonym "Angelus Silesius" for his *Der Cherubinischer Wandersmann* (The Cherub Wanderer), a collection of epigrammatic mystical verses? "Agesilaus," though a real and not a made-up name, seems to scramble "Angelus Silesius" into a single word, and Santander could suggest the mixed Santa/ Satanic quality of Benjamin the pilgrim or some desired relation to Southern (Spanish and Kabbalistic) rather than Northern spirit of place through the name of this town.

What we are given, then, is the aura of a name: "Agesilaus Santander" is the quintessence of an anagram rather than a univocally decipherable writing. The scrambling is permanent and the meanings we recover are fugitive constructions, like the "new angels" in contrast to the old. The name may even accuse the maker of the name: it is "satanic" also in that. For it stands as the product of an artificial mysticism that evokes an "aura artificiel" in the manner of Baudelaire's "paradis artificiel." It betrays a fallen aura, mere aroma of aura, the whiff of a Turkish cigarette and eastern mysteries. Like "Xanadu" and "Kubla Khan" the name is an authentic fake, a given or proper name consumed by the imagination, the scar of a signature that belongs to no one. "Its traits had no human likeness." Benjamin's fantasy could be part of a book on Hashish he meant to write. He continued to look, patiently and yet in flight, to the origin of all names in the garden God had planted eastward of Eden. Psychoanalysis: the Eden connection.

BIBLIOGRAPHICAL NOTE

Translations from Jacques Derrida's *Glas* (Paris: Galilée, 1974) are my own. The reference after each quotation is to the page and column (a left, b right) of *Glas*. Several essays by Lacan are available in translation; Antony Wilden's *The Language of the Self* (Baltimore: The Johns Hopkins University Press, 1968), contains a fully annotated version of the famous "Discours de Rome." I quote from Wilden's translation on pp. 89 and 105 above. A fine Lacanian study, directly focused on literature and relevant to *Glas*, is that of J. Laplanche, *Hölderlin et la question du père* (Paris: Presses Universitaires de France, 1961). Other analysts, influenced by Lacan or D. W. Winnicott or both, who have done work to interest English readers, are André Green and J.-B. Pontalis.

Sartre's book on Genet, originally published in 1952, is translated by Bernard Frechtman as *Saint Genet: Actor and Martyr* (New York: G. Braziller, 1963). I refer chiefly to the section "A Dizzying Word" in book 1, which contains the story of Genet's "specular capture" (Lacan's, not Sartre's, phrase) by the identity-imposing words "You are a thief." Freud's remarks on the "language of flowers" in *The Interpretation of Dreams* are found in the Standard Edition of the *Complete Psychological Works* (London: Hogarth Press, 1953-74), 4: 319-25, and 5: 652: see also pp. 374-77. Sandor Ferenczi's bioanalysis is his *Thalassa: Toward a Theory of Genitality*, first published in German in 1924. An important step in the French reception of the book was Nicolas Abraham's edition for the "Petite Bibliothèque Payot" in 1962.

On wounding and naming, see L. Brisman, "'At Thy Word'": A Reading of *Romeo and Juliet*," *Bulletin of the Midwest MLA* 8 (1975): 21-35; also Norman Holland, "A Touching of Literary and Psychiatric Education," *Seminars in Psychiatry* 5 (1973): 287-99. On the psychic import of names, the following sources may prove interesting: Sigmund Freud, *Totem and Taboo*, ch. 4, the section on "Nominalist Theories;" Karl Abraham's short essay of 1911, "Über die determinierende Kraft des Namens." Jean Starobinski has edited Saussure's notebooks, recovering his theory of the anagrammatic (hypogrammatic) generation of certain hermetic verses (*Les Mots sous les mots* [Paris: Gallimard, 1971]). See also Jacques Derrida, *De la grammatologie* (Paris: Editions Minuit, 1967), pp. 157 ff., "La Guerre des noms propres." This book has been translated by G. Spivak as *Of Grammatology* (Baltimore: The Johns Hopkins University Press, 1976). Also Dwight Culler, *Tennyson* (New Haven: Yale University Press, 1977), ch. 1, "Tennyson, Tennyson, Tennyson." The amphibious relations between proper and common nouns are deepened by the work of Nicolas Abraham and Maria Torok on cryptonomy in *Le Verbier de l'homme aux loups* (Paris: Aubier-Flammarion, 1976). This is preceded by "Fors," an essay by Derrida translated in *Georgia Review* 31 (1977): 64-120.

Gershom Scholem's "Walter Benjamin und sein Engel," containing the *Agesilaus Santander* text in its two versions, is found in *Zur Aktualität Walter Benjamins*, ed. Siegfried Unseld (Frankfurt am Main: Suhrkamp, 1972). I quote the second version of Benjamin's text and have modified the translation by W. J. Dannhauser in *Denver Quarterly* 9 (1974): 9-12. There is some wordplay that cannot be rendered in translation; it includes perhaps an allusion to the fact that as a name "Walter Benjamin" seems to contain two first names (Benjamin, the family name, being also a common first name). The German word for first name, "Vorname" is homophonous with "Vornahme," that is, "project" or "resolution." Benjamin's concept of the "aura" is described at length in *The Work of Art in the Era of Its Mechanical Reproduction*, originally published in 1936.

Jacques Derrida

Coming into One's Own

Translated by James Hulbert

KEEPING IT IN THE FAMILY

Despite the richness and novelty of the content brought forward in the second chapter of *Beyond the Pleasure Principle*, despite numerous marching orders and steps forward, not an inch of ground is gained: there is no decision and not the slightest progress in the question that concerns the speculator, the question of the PP as absolute master. Nevertheless, this chapter is often remembered as one of the most important, the most decisive of the essay—particularly because of the story of the wooden reel and the *fort/da*. And since the repetition compulsion is associated with the death drive and a repetition compulsion seems to dominate the episode of the wooden reel, some feel that they can connect this story to the discussion and even the proof of the existence of a death drive. It means they haven't *read* the text: the speculator retains nothing of this *fort/da*, at least not in his proof about something beyond the PP. He claims that he can still explain the *fort/da* completely in the domain and under the authority of the PP. And he actually succeeds in doing so. It is indeed the story of the PP that he tells us, an important moment in his own genealogy, but a moment of himself.

Not that this chapter is devoid of interest, nor that the anecdote about the wooden reel has no bearing. Quite to the contrary: perhaps its bearing is just not inscribed in the register of *proof*, whose most obvious string[1] is held by the question of whether "we" psychoanalysts are right in *believing* in the absolute domination of the PP. Where, then, is the bearing of the wooden reel inscribed?

If we consider the argumentative framework of the chapter,

we notice that something repeats itself, and this process of repetition must be identified not only in the content (the examples, the materials described and analyzed) but also in Freud's very writing, in the "steps" taken by his text, in what it does as well as in what it says, in its "acts" as much as in its "objects." What obviously repeats itself in this chapter is the movement of the speculator to reject, set aside, make disappear (*fort*), defer everything that seems to call the PP into question. He notes that it is not enough, that he must postpone the question. Then he summons back the hypothesis of something beyond the pleasure principle only to dismiss it again. The hypothesis returns only like something that has not really returned but has merely passed into the ghost of its presence.

Let's begin with the "normal" and "primeval": the child, in the typical activity that is attributed to him—play. It appears to be an activity wholly subjugated to the PP (and indeed we shall see that such is the case and that it is wholly under the surveillance of a PP that is, however, tormented or shaped by his/its silent other)[2] —an activity, moreover, as independent as possible of the second principle, the PR.

And this is what I shall call the argument of the wooden reel: a legendary argument that is neither story nor history nor myth nor fiction. Nor is it the systematic elaboration of a theoretical proof. It is fragmentary, without conclusion, selective: rather an argument in the sense of an outline. And this legend is already too legendary, overloaded, obliterated. In the face of the immense literature whose investment [*investissement*; also "cathexis"] this legendary argument has attracted, I should like to undertake a partial and naive reading, as naive and spontaneous as possible.

Here for the first time in this book is a passage that appears to be autobiographical and even domestic. This fact is veiled, but all the more significant. Freud says that he was a witness—an *interested* witness—to the experiment. It took place in his family,

though he does not mention this. We know from other sources
that the interested witness was none other than the child's
grandfather.[3] Even if an experiment could ever be restricted to
observation, the conditions as they are defined in this account
were not those of an observation. The experimental conditions
here, supposedly those of adequate observation ("It was more
than a mere fleeting observation, for I lived under the same roof
as the child and his parents" [p. 8]), guarantee the observation
only by turning the observer into a participant. But what part
did he play? Can he decide his part himself? Neither the question of objectivity nor any epistemological question in canonical form has the slightest pertinence, for the very good reason
that this experiment and the account of it claim to be nothing
less than a genealogy of objectivity in general. How, then, can
they be judged by the tribunal whose founding they repeat?
But, inversely, what right does anyone have to forbid a tribunal
to judge the conditions under which it is established, or to judge
the account that an interested witness, a participant, gives of
that establishment? Especially if the witness shows every sign of
being strangely busy: busy, for example, producing the institution of his desire, making it the start of his own genealogy,
making the tribunal and the legal tradition his heritage, his to
delegate, his legacy, *his own.*[4]

The account that we have is first sifted, pruned, deliberately
restricted. This discrimination is in part declared at the outset.
The speculator, who does not say that he has actually started to
speculate yet, admits that he did not wish to "include the whole
field covered by these phenomena" (p. 8). He has retained only
those traits that were pertinent from the economic point of
view. "Economic": we can already translate by playing a little
(play is not yet forbidden at this phase of the origin of everything, of the present, the object, language, work, earnestness,
and so forth) but not gratuitously from the viewpoint of the
oikos [literally, "house"], the law of the *oikos*, of that which is

one's own as one's own household[*domestico-familial*], and even, as we shall see in the same way, as one's own house-of-mourning [*domestico-funéraire*]. The speculating grandfather justifies the accounts that he is giving and the discrimination that he openly performs in them, by referring to the economic point of view. It has thus far been neglected in the "different theories of children's play," and it constitutes the privileged starting point for *Beyond the Pleasure Principle*, for what the one who keeps or gives the accounts is in the process of doing, i.e., of writing.

> These theories attempt to discover the motives which lead children to play, but they fail to bring into the foreground the *economic* motive, the consideration of the yield of pleasure involved. Without wishing to include the whole field covered by these phenomena, I have been able, through a chance opportunity which presented itself, to throw some light upon the first game played by a little boy of one and a half and created by himself [*selbstgeschaffen*]. It was more than a mere fleeting observation, for I lived under the same roof as the child and his parents for some weeks, and it was some time before I discovered the meaning of the puzzling activity which he constantly repeated. [P. 8]

From this first paragraph of the account onward, a single trait characterizes the object of observation, the action of the game: repetition, repeated repetition [*das andauernd wiederholte Tun*]. That's all. The other characteristic, "puzzling," doesn't describe anything; it is empty, but with an emptiness that calls out and that, like every puzzle, calls for a story.

You may say: wait, there is another descriptive trait in this first paragraph. The game, which constitutes the repetition of repetition, is "*selbstgeschaffen*," a game that the child brought about or let come about by himself or by itself, spontaneously, and it is the first of this sort. But none of this (spontaneity, self-production, the primeval quality of the first time) contributes any descriptive content that does not go back to the self-engendering of self-repetition: the heterotautology (the definition of the speculative in Hegel)[5] of repeated repetition, of self-repetition, in its pure form, which will constitute the game.

There is repetition between pleasure and displeasure, repetition of a pleasure and a displeasure, whose (pleasant/unpleasant) content is not an external aid to repetition but an inner determination, the object of an analytical predication. The possibility of this analytical predication will gradually develop the hypothesis of a "drive" that is more primeval than the PP and independent of the PP. The PP will be surpassed, is already surpassed in advance, by the speculation that he/it incites and by his/its own repetition.

Superpose what the grandfather says his grandson does, with all the earnestness that befits an elder grandson named Ernst (the importance of being earnest)—but not Ernst Freud, for the movement of this genealogy passes by way of the daughter, who is also a wife, i.e., who perpetuates the race only by risking the name (I'll let you follow the rounds of this factor[6] until it reaches all those women about whom it's hard to know whether they kept the movement without the name or lost the movement in order to keep, or because they had kept, the name; I advise only that in the question of the analytic "movement" as the genealogy of the son-in-law, you not forget Judaic law)—superpose what he says that his grandson does earnestly on what he is doing himself in saying so, in writing *Beyond the Pleasure Principle*, in playing so earnestly (in speculating) at writing it. For the speculative heterotautology of the thing is that that "beyond" is lodged in the repetition of repetition of the PP.

Superpose: *he* (the grandson of his grandfather, the grandfather of his grandson) repeats repetition compulsively, but it all never goes anywhere, never advances by a single step. He repeats an operation that consists of pretending to dispatch pleasure, the object of pleasure or the pleasure principle, represented here by the wooden reel that is supposed to represent the mother (and/or, we shall see, the father, in place of the son-in-law, the father as son-in-law [*le père en gendre*], the other family name), to bring it back again and again. He pretends to dispatch the PP in order to make it return endlessly, in order to note that it comes back of its own accord and to conclude: it is always there—I am always there. *Da*. The PP retains total authority, has never been away.

In every detail we can see the superposition of the subsequent description of the *fort/da* (on the grandson's side of the house of Freud) with the description of the speculative game, itself so assiduous and so repetitive, of the grandfather in writing *Beyond the Pleasure Principle*. It's not, strictly speaking, a matter of superposition, nor of parallelism, nor of analogy, nor of coincidence. The necessity that links the two descriptions is of a different sort: we shall not find it easy to give a name to it, but it is clearly the main thing at stake for me in the sifting, interested reading that I am repeating here. Who summons whom to return in this double *fort/da* that couples in the same genealogical (and conjugal) writing both the story and the one who is telling it (the "earnest" grandson's game with the wooden reel and the grandfather's earnest speculation with the PP)?

This simple question, left unanswered, suggests that the description of the earnest game of Ernst, the elder grandson of the grandfather of psychoanalysis, no longer must be read *only* as a theoretical argument, a strictly theoretical speculation that tends to conclude that what we have here is the repetition compulsion *or* the death drive *or* simply an inner limit to the PP (you know that Freud, whatever his allies and his opponents on this issue have claimed, never comes to a definitive conclusion about this). Rather, the description of Ernst's game can also be read as an autobiography of Freud; not merely an auto-biography entrusting his life to his own more or less testamentary writing but a more or less living description of his own writing, of his way of writing *Beyond the Pleasure Principle* in particular. It is not merely a superposition or a tautological reversal or mirror—as would be the case if Freud wrote down what his descendants dictated and thus held the first pen, the pen that is always passed from hand to hand; if Freud made a return to Freud by the mediation of his grandson. The auto-biography of *writing* at once posits and deposes, in the same motion, the psychoanalytic movement. I'll wager that this double *fort/da* cooperates in initiating the cause of psychoanalysis, in setting in motion the psychoanalytic "movement," in being that movement. If there lingers in the astounding event of this cooperation the unanalyzed remnant of an unconscious, if this remnant shapes and constructs with its otherness the auto-biography of this testamentary writing, then I wager that it will be handed down blindly by the entire movement of the return to Freud. The remnant that silently shapes the scene of that cooperation is doubtless unreadable, but it defines the sole urgency, the sole interest, of what remains to be done.

I have never wished to overuse the abyss, nor above all the abyss structure [*mise en abyme*].[7] I have no strong belief in it, I distrust the confidence that it, at bottom, inspires, and I find it too representational to go far enough, not to *avoid* the very thing into which it pretends to plunge us. What does the appearance here of a certain *mise en abyme* open on, and close around? This appearance is not immediately apparent, but it must have played a secret role in the fascination that this little story of the reel exerts upon the reader—this anecdote that might have been thought banal, paltry, fragmented, told in passing and without the slightest bearing, if we are to believe the very man who reports it. Yet the story that he reports seems to place the writing of the report into an abyss structure: what is reported has a bearing on the one who reports it. The site of what is readable, as the origin of writing, is borne away. Nothing can be set down in writing any more. The value of repetition "*en abyme*" of Freud's writing is in a relationship of structural mimesis to the relationship between the PP and "his"/"its" death drive. Once again, this drive is not opposed to the PP, but

it etches into the PP with a testamentary writing *"en abyme."*
Such is presumably the "movement," in the irreducible novelty
of its repetition, in the utterly singular event of its double
relationship.

If we were to simplify the question, it would become, for
example, how can an auto-biographical writing, in the abyss of
an unterminated self-analysis, give *its* birth to a world institution? And how does the interruption or the limit of the self-
analysis, cooperating in rather than impeding the *mise en abyme*,
reproduce its mark in the institutionalization of psychoanalysis,
in such a way that the possibility of this re-mark does not cease
to produce offspring, multiplying the progeny of its splits,
conflicts, divisions, alliances, marriages, and verifications?

Such is the speculation that characterizes this auto-biography;
but rather than simplify the question, this time we should
approach the process from the other direction and stress its
apparent premise: what is auto-biography if all its consequences
(as I have just enumerated them) are thus possible? Remember,
Freud, the first and thus the only one to have undertaken, if
not defined, self-analysis, did not himself know what it was.

To move on in my reading, I now have need of an essential
possibility that fortune, if that's the word for it, turned into an
event: all auto-biographical speculation, insofar as it constitutes
a legacy and the institution of a movement without limits, must
take into account, at the very moment of speculation, the
mortality of the legatees. As soon as there is mortality, then in
principle death can come at any moment. Thus the speculator
can survive the legatee, and this possibility is inscribed in the
structure of the legacy, and even in the extreme case of self-
analysis. Untimely death and the silent state of the legatee: this
is one of the possibilities of what dictates and makes the writer
write—even the one who seems not to have written, Socrates, or
the one whose writing is supposed to duplicate discourse or
listening (Freud and certain others). So one gives oneself one's

own movement, inheriting from oneself: it's set up so that the ghost, at least, can always collect. All he has to do is to pronounce a name as the guarantee of a signature.

It happened to Freud and to certain others, but the fact that the event takes place on the stage of the world is not in itself enough to illustrate the possibility of its happening.

And what follows is not merely an example.

One daughter is silent. Unlike a daughter who would make use of her father's name and influence in a lengthy discourse about who inherits what, the silent daughter seems perhaps to say, "Here's why your father has the word." Not only "my father," but "your father." Her name is Sophie: Freud's daughter, Ernst's mother, whose death knell will sound soon enough in the text—soft and low, in a strange note added after the fact.

THE NAME GAME

I shall resume Freud's account precisely where I left it, without omitting anything. He insists that the child is normal, a necessary condition for a relevant experiment. He is a model child, and thus his intellectual development is marked by no unseemly precociousness. He gets along beautifully with everyone.

Especially with his mother.

(I leave it to you, following the pattern already elaborated, to relate the content of the story to the scene of its writing, here, for example, switching the places of the narrator and the main character, or the couple, Ernst and Sophie, the third one (the father/husband/son-in-law) never being far away and sometimes even too close. In a traditional story [*récit classique*], the narrator, the supposed observer, is not the same as the author. If it were not different in this case (since what we have here is not presented as literary fiction), it would be—it will be—necessary to go over the distinction again between the "I" of the narrator and the "I" of the author, adapting it to a new "meta-psychological" topography.)

Ernst, I was saying, gets along well with everyone—especially his mother, since he didn't cry when she was away. She would leave him for hours. Why didn't he cry? Freud seems pleased and at the same time surprised, even sorry. In the very sentence in which he ascribes to excellence of character the fact that his grandson didn't cry for his daughter (his mother) during such long absences, he adds "*obwohl*" ("even though"), even though he was very much attached to her; she had not only nursed him but had also never had anyone else in to care for him. But this small anomaly is soon passed over: Freud never follows up on the "*obwohl*." Everything is fine, wonderful child, *but*. Here's the "but": this wonderful child had one disturbing habit. It's hard to see right off how Freud, at the end of the amazing description of it that he offers, can calmly conclude: "I eventually realized that it was a game."

> The child was not at all precocious in his intellectual development. At the age of one and a half he could say only a few comprehensible words; he could also make use of a number of meaningful sounds that were intelligible to those around him. He was, however, on good terms with his parents and their one servant-girl, and he was praised for being a "good little boy." He did not disturb his parents at night, he conscientiously obeyed orders not to touch certain objects . . . and above all he never cried when his mother left him for hours, even though he was greatly attached to this mother, who had not only nursed him herself but had also looked after him without any outside help. [P. 8, translation modified]

There seems to be no shadow to mar this scene, no "but." There are a "however" and an "even though," stabilizers, inner compensations that describe a situation in equilibrium. He was by no means precocious (to the contrary, if anything), *but* his relations with his parents were fine; he didn't cry when his mother walked out on him, *but* he was attached to her, and no wonder. Do I alone detect a suppressed accusation here? Freud cannot help making excuses for his daughter's son. So what does he have to reproach him for?

The big "but" comes right after all this, yet the word "but" does not appear. It is replaced by a "now" (*nun*): "Now, this good little boy had on occasion a disturbing habit" (p. 8, translation modified). The good qualities (in spite of everything) of this fine boy, his normality, his calm, his ability to put up with that beloved daughter (mother), no tears, no fears—it's pretty clear that all this is going to cost something. Everything here is elaborately structured, bolstered, governed by a system of rules and compensations, an economy that will appear shortly in the form of a bad habit. And that bad habit makes it possible for him to bear what the "good" ones cost him: the boy is a speculator, too. What does he pay (what does he purchase) when he obeys the order not to touch "certain objects"? How does the PP negotiate between good habits and bad? The grandfather, father of the mother and of the daughter, deliberately chooses the descriptive traits. I can see him anxious, under pressure, like a playwright or director who must act a part in his own play. In preparing the play, he hastens to be sure that everything is in order, then rushes to get into his costume. This takes the form of a dogmatic authoritarianism, unexpected decisions, interrupted sentences, questions that go unanswered. The stage is set, the actor-playwright-producer has done everything himself, and the curtain is about to go up. But we don't know whether it rises *on* the scene or *in* the scene. Before any of the characters appear, there is a curtained bed. In essence, entering or leaving means passing by that curtain.

(I leave it to you to raise this curtain on all the other words and things—curtains, canvasses, veils, screens, hymens, umbrellas, etc.—that have concerned me for so long.)

> Now, this good little boy had on occasion a disturbing habit of taking any small objects he could get hold of and throwing them far away

from him into a corner, under the bed, and so on, so that hunting for
his toys and picking them up again [*das Zusammensuchen seines Spiel-
zeuges*] was often no easy chore. [P. 8, translation modified]

Gathering, collecting for the purpose of returning: this is what
the grandfather calls work, a chore, and often a difficult one.
On the other hand, scattering, sending things far away, he calls
a game, playing, and the objects that are moved he calls toys,
playthings, *Spielzeug*. The whole process is divided, not in a
division of labor but in a division between work and play, between the child's play and the parents' (often difficult) work.
Why does he scatter everything he gets hold of, and *who* is
scattering, dispatching, *what*?

The wooden reel has yet to appear. In a certain sense, it will
be merely an example of the operation that Freud has just
described—but an exemplary example, occasioning a supplementary "observation" that will be decisive for Freud's interpretation. The child throws and retrieves, scatters and gathers, gives
and takes all by himself: he combines scattering and gathering,
the different roles, work and play, in one participant, it seems,
and one object. This is what the grandfather calls "a game,"
when all the strings are brought together and held in one hand,
with the parents needed neither as workers nor as players.

So far the *Spielzeug* in question has been a collective: all the
toys, the unity of a dispersible multiplicity, which the parents'
task is to gather up again and which the grandfather gathers
together in a single word.[8] This collective unity is the equipment for a game that can become *dislocated*: moved and fragmented or scattered. If the child parts with his *Spielzeug* as if
with himself and for the purpose of being gathered up and put
back together, it is because he, too, is a collective, and the
reassembly of that collective can give rise to a whole new range
of combinations. Everyone who plays or works at gathering up
the pieces has a piece of the game. Not that Freud says so, but
he will say, in one of the two notes I've mentioned, that what in

the child's "game" appears and disappears does indeed include the child himself or his image. He is part of his *Spielzeug*.

The wooden reel is still to come, after this interpretative anticipation: as he threw all his *Spielzeug* far away,

> he gave vent to a loud, long-drawn-out "o-o-o-o," accompanied by an expression of interest and satisfaction. His mother and the observer were agreed in thinking that [*nach dem übereinstimmenden Urteil*] this was not a mere interjection but represented the German word "*fort*" ["gone"]. I eventually realized that it was a game and that the only use he made of any of his toys was to play "gone" [*fortsein*] with them. [Pp. 8-9, translation modified]

Freud's intervention (I don't say the grandfather's, but that of the one who narrates what was experienced by the observer, the one who finally realized that "it was a game"; there are at least three agencies or personae of the same "subject": the speculator-narrator, the observer, and the grandfather, who is never explicitly identified with the other two by the other two, and so forth)—Freud's intervention, I say, merits special attention. He says that as observer he also interpreted—and *named*. Now what he calls a game, rather than work (work being the chore of gathering up what has been scattered), is, paradoxically, the operation that consists in not playing with one's toys: he used the toys (we are told) only to play that he was sending them far away. The "game" thus consists in not playing with one's toys but making them serve another function, i.e., *Fortsein*. Such would be the deflection, redirection, or *teleological* purposiveness of this game. But teleology, purposiveness of *Fortsein*, in view of what, of whom? What and who are served by this utilization of what ordinarily presents itself as gratuitous or useless, i.e., play, a game? Perhaps this nongratuitousness brings not one *single* benefit, and perhaps not a *benefit*, and perhaps not to a single person or agent of speculation. There is a tele-ology of the operation that is being interpreted and a teleology of interpretation. And there is more than one interpreter: the grandfather (our observer), the speculator and father of psychoanalysis (our narrator), and then, linked to each of these, the woman whose judgment, we are told, corroborates and coincides with her father's interpretation to such an extent that they can be superposed.

This concurrence linking father and daughter in the interpretation of the "o-o-o-o" as *"fort"* is unusual in several ways. It is hard to imagine the scene in detail, or even to credit its existence. Still, Freud does tell us that the boy's mother and the observer have somehow come together to make the *same* judgment about the meaning of the sound that their son and grandson made in their presence, indeed *for* them. There's no telling what the source of such an identification is. But you can be sure that wherever it comes from, it links the three characters in what we must now more than ever call the *same* speculation. In secret, they have all named the same thing.

Freud never stops to wonder about the language into which he translates the *o/a*. To recognize in those sounds a semantic content linked to a specific language (a certain opposition of German words) and from there a semantic content that goes beyond that language (the interpretation of the child's behavior) is a process that requires complex theoretical procedures. We may suspect that the *o/a* is not restricted merely to a formal opposition of values, the content of which may vary freely. If this variation is restricted (as we must conclude from the fact—if it concerns us—that the father and the daughter and the mother find themselves united in the same semantic reading), then we can state the following hypothesis: there is a proper name involved in those sounds, whether we mean this figuratively (every signified whose signifier can neither vary nor be translated into another signifier without loss of significance, suggests a proper-name effect) or literally.

And what if this perfect concurrence in the judgment handed down (*Urteil*) were what the son, i.e., the grandson, was after, if it were moreover what he believed in without knowing, without wanting to believe it? The father is far away, *fort*—that is, *one* of the two fathers, the father of the little boy. As for Sophie's father, the father of psychoanalysis, he's still there.

The wooden reel still has not appeared. Here it is, as the text continues:

> One day I made an observation which confirmed my view. The child had a wooden reel [*Holzspule*; French, *bobine en bois*] with a piece of string tied round it. It never occurred to him to pull it along the floor behind him, for instance, and play at its being a carriage [*Wagen mit ihr zu spielen*]. What he did was to hold the reel by the string and very skilfully throw it over the edge of his little curtained [or "veiled"] bed, so that it disappeared into it, at the same time uttering his meaningful "o-o-o-o." He then pulled the reel out of the bed again by the string and hailed its reappearance with a joyful *"da"* ["there"]. This, then, was the complete game—disappearance and return. As a rule one witnessed only its first act, which was repeated untiringly as a game in itself, though there is no doubt that the greater pleasure was attached to the second act. [P. 9, translation modified]

At the end of this last sentence, there is a footnote to which we shall come in a moment.

"This, then," says Freud, "was the complete game." Which implies immediately: this, then, is the complete observation, and the complete interpretation, of that game. If the completeness were obvious and certain, would Freud insist upon it, would he point it out as if it were necessary to close that completeness in all haste? We suspect all the more that the object or its description is incomplete because (1) the scene is that of an endlessly repeated supplementation, as if it could never become complete, and so on, and (2) there is something like an incompleteness axiom in the structure of the writing scene, owing to the position of the speculator as an interested observer. Even if completeness were possible, it would never appear to such an "observer," nor could he declare it to be complete.

But these are generalities. They outline only the formal conditions for determinate incompleteness, the significant absence of some especially pertinent characteristic—either in the scene described or in the description or in the unconscious that links them, their common inherited unconscious, telecommunicated in accordance with the same teleology.

Freud says that the greater pleasure, although it is observed less directly, is the *Wiederkommen*, the return, the coming again. Yet what becomes itself again by coming again (like a ghost) must be dispatched once more, again and again, if the game is to be complete.

The game *is* complete, he says. Yet he seems surprised and indicates a definite regret that it never occurred to the good little boy to pull the reel behind him and play *Wagen* (carriage, car, train) with it. It's as if the speculator (whose phobia for railroads is well enough known to put us on the right track) would have played train himself with one of those "small objects." This is the first query, the first perplexity, of the father of the object or the grandfather of the subject, of the father of the daughter (the mother, Ernst's object) or of the grandfather of the little boy (Ernst as "subject" of the *fort/da*). Why doesn't he play train or car? Wouldn't that be more normal? If he had been playing in his grandson's place (thus with his daughter, since the reel represents her, as he says in the next paragraph), the (grand)father would have played train (please grant me all these parentheses—the (grand)father, the daughter (mother)— they are necessary to indicate the blurred syntax of the genealogical scene, the fact that all the places are occupied, and the ultimate origin of what I have called the athetic nature [*l'athèse*] of *Beyond the Pleasure Principle*);[9] and since the game is in earnest, it would then have been even more so, he says earnestly, but it never occurred to Ernst. Instead of playing on the ground, Ernst insisted on bringing the bed into the game, on playing with the thing over the bed but also in the bed. (Contrary to what many readers have gathered from the text and its translation, the child is not in the bed, it seems, when he throws the reel.) From outside the bed he throws the reel over the edge of the bed, over the veils or curtains that surround the edge; he pulls the car "out of the bed" to bring it back—*da*. Thus the bed is *fort*, which contradicts, perhaps, all desire.

What is playing train, for the (grand)father? Speculating: it would be never throwing the thing (but does the child ever throw it without having it on a string?), keeping it constantly at a distance, but the same distance (since the length of the string is constant), making or letting it move at the same time and with the same rhythm as oneself. This train never even has to return, for it never really leaves. The speculating grandfather makes sure of [*assure*; also "insures"] the thing only by depriving himself of a supplementary pleasure, the very one that he describes as the main one for Ernst, i.e., the second act, the return. He deprives himself of it to spare himself the pain or risk of the wager. And so as not to bring the desired bed into play.

If the child is indeed outside the bed but near it, concerned with the bed, which his grandfather seems to reproach him for, then the curtains, the veils, the fabric that hides the bars, do form the inner partition of the *fort/da*, the double screen that divides the *fort/da* on the inside, with its inner and outer faces, but only by gathering it with itself, pricking it twice, to itself— *fort:da*. This I call the *hymen* of the *fort:da*. The veil is the interesting thing about the bed and the *fort:da* of all these generations.

The grandfather regrets that his grandson never had these ideas (wise or crazy) of a game without a bed, but they didn't fail to occur to *him*. He even finds them natural, just the thing to improve the description, if not the game. In the same way, we might say, he regrets that his grandson did have the ideas that he had for him.

Was this bed, finally, with its so very necessary and so very

indeterminate edge, a *couch*? Not quite, despite all the Orphism
of speculation. And yet . . .

What the speculating (grand)father calls the complete game
would be the game in the duality of its two phases: disappearing
and coming back, absence and re-presentation. What links the
game to itself is the *re-* of the return, the extra turn of repetition and reappearing. He insists that the greater quantity of
pleasure is attached to the second phase, to the *re*-turn that
determines everything, and without which nothing would come
about. This permits us to anticipate that this operation, in its
so-called "complete" totality, will come entirely under the
authority of the PP. Far from being thwarted by repetition, the
PP will also seek to recall in the repetition of appearing, of
presence, of a repetition, as we shall see, that is mastered and
that verifies and confirms the mastery that constitutes it (that
of the PP). The mastery of the PP is none other than mastery
in general; rather than the *Herrschaft* ["mastery"] of the PP,
there is simply *Herrschaft* that *leaves* itself only to reappropriate itself, to *come* into its own (self)—a tautoteleology that,
however, makes or lets the other return as his/its household
ghost. It is thus predictable. What returns comes neither to contradict nor to oppose the PP but to erode it/him as its/his own
other [*étranger*], to hollow out an abyss in the PP, starting
from a primevalness more primeval than the PP and independent of it/him, older yet in it/him: not, under the name of
death drive or repetition compulsion, *another master* or an
antimaster [*contre-maître*; cf. *contremaître*, "overseer"] but
something other than mastery, entirely different. But whereas
it is entirely different, it must not oppose, must not enter into
a dialectical relationship with the master (life, the PP *as* life,
living, alive), e.g., a master-slave dialectic. Nor must this non-
mastery enter into a dialectical relationship with death, e.g., to
become, as in speculative idealism, the "true master."

I do indeed say, the PP as mastery in general. At this point in our discussion, the supposed "complete game" no longer involves this or that specific object, e.g., the wooden reel or what it replaces. What's involved is the *re-* in general, returning in general, and disappearance/reappearance; not some object that goes out and comes back but the very going and returning, in other words the self-presentation of re-presentation, the self-returning of returning. This happens also to the object that becomes again the subject of the *fort:da*, the disappearance and reappearance of *oneself*, the object coming back into *his own*, himself.

And thus we come to the first of the two footnotes. It is a note to "the second act," to which "the greater pleasure" is said to be undoubtedly attached. What does the note say? That the child stages the usefulness of the *fort:da* with something that is no longer an object-object, an extra reel [*bobine*] replacing something else, but with a replacement *bobine* for the replacement *bobine*, with his own *bobine* ["noggin"], with himself as subject-object in the mirror and without the mirror. Here is the note:

> A further observation subsequently confirmed this interpretation fully. One day the child's mother had been away for several hours and on her return was met with the words "Baby o-o-o-o!" which was at first incomprehensible. It soon turned out, however, that during this long period of solitude the child had found a method of making *himself* disappear. He had discovered his reflection in a full-length mirror which did not quite reach to the ground, so that by crouching down he could make his mirror-image "gone" [*fort*]. [P. 9, n. 1]

The child identifies with the mother, because he disappears like her and makes her return along with himself, by making himself return without making anything else return but himself, her in him(her)self. This he manages while remaining in the closest proximity to the PP; the PP never leaves, and it/he gives (gets) the greatest pleasure at this moment. He makes himself disappear, he masters himself symbolically, and he makes him-

self reappear from then on without the mirror, in his very disappearance, keeping himself (like his mother) on a string, on the
wire. He makes himself *re-*, still in accordance with the law of
the PP, in the grand speculation of a PP that seems never to
leave him/itself, nor anyone. This recalling, by telephone or
teletype [i.e., voice or writing, from afar] , produces the "movement" by contracting itself, by signing a contract with itself.

TAKING THE TOLL: THE FREUDIAN RING
AND THE THEME OF THE THREE (?) CASKETS

The earnest game of *fort:da* links absence and presence in the
re- of returning. It sets up repetition as their relationship,
relating them to each other, bringing them together, bringing
one to bear on (or under) the other. Thus, the game means playing *usefully* with oneself as with one's own object. This confirms the abysslike relationship that I was proposing earlier:
between on the one hand the object or the content of *Beyond
the Pleasure Principle*, what Freud is supposedly writing, describing, analyzing, examining, treating, and so forth, and on the
other hand the system of his writing acts, the writing scene that
he stages or that is played out. This is the "complete game" of
the *fort:da*. With(out) the object of his text, Freud does exactly
what Ernst does with(out) his *bobine*. And if the game is called
complete in each case, we must envisage a highly symbolic completeness formed from the completeness of each, a completeness incomplete in each of its parts, thus completely incomplete
when each completeness is related to the other and they multiply, supplementing each other without completing each other.
Let's grant that Freud writes. He writes that he writes; he describes what he describes, which, however, is also what he is
doing; he is doing what he describes, i.e., what Ernst does: he
goes *fort:da* with his *bobine*. Each time that we say "do," we

should be more precise: "make" or "let" happen (*lassen*). Freud's *fort:da* is not performed, tirelessly, with that object that is the PP: just as Ernst, in recalling the object (mother, plaything, or whatever), comes also to recall *himself* in an immediately supplementary operation, in the same way the speculating grandfather, describing or recalling this or that, recalls *himself*, and produces what is called his text, making a contract with himself so as to be left holding all the strings of his line, descendants and ascendants, in an incontestable *ascendancy*. If something is incontestable, it also requires no witnesses, yet one cannot help acquiescing in it: no opposing testimony seems capable of measuring up in the face of this teleological self-institution. The snare is in place, and you can't pull on one string without getting your hand caught, or your foot, or the rest of you, in this lasso, this *lacet* ["snare," but also "shoelace," "corset lace," etc.].[10] Freud didn't set up the snare, but he found out how to go about it [*il a su s'y prendre*; literally, "how to get caught in it"]. But we have said nothing yet, we know nothing, about this knowledge, for he himself was surprised by the catch [*par la prise*]. He was unable to grasp it all or foresee it all.

This is expressed first of all in an utterly formal, general way, in a sort of a priori writing. The *fort:da* scene, whatever its exemplary content, is always in the process of describing, in advance, the scene of its own description. Since the objects of the *fort:da* can be substituted for one another so as to lay bare the substitutional structure itself, the formal structure becomes readable: it is no longer a matter of the dispatching that renders this or that absent and then of the bringing near that renders this or that present; it is a matter of the distance of what is far away and the nearness of what is nearby, the absence of what is absent or the presence of what is present.

Freud recalls—his memories and himself. (Like Ernst in the mirror and without it.) But Freud's speculative writing also recalls—something else and itself. And above all, what mirrors seem to offer is not, as is often believed, merely getting back what is one's own, any more than in the case of the *da*.

The speculator recalls himself, but we cannot know whether this "himself" can say "I, me, myself"; and even if he said "myself," what self or ego would then assume the authority of speech. The *fort:da* alone should rob us of any assurance about this. This is why, if we must have recourse here to the autobiographical, it must be in an entirely new way. This text is auto-biographical, but in a completely different way from what was believed before. First, auto-biography is not exactly the same as self-analysis. Second, it will force us to reconsider the whole topography of the *autos*, the self. Finally, far from reassuring us about our familiar knowledge about what autobiography means, it sets up, with its own strange contract, a new theoretical and practical charter for every possible autobiography.

Beyond the Pleasure Principle is thus not an *example* of what we believe we already know under the name of auto-biography. It writes the autobiographical, and, from the fact that an "author" recounts something of his life in it, we can no longer conclude that the document is without truth value, without value as science or as philosophy. A "domain" opens up in which the "inscription" of a subject in his text is also the necessary condition for the pertinence and performance of a text, for its "worth" beyond what is called empirical subjectivity (if, indeed, there is such a thing, since subjectivity speaks, writes, and substitutes one object for another, substitutes and adds itself as an object for and to another). The notion of truth value is utterly incapable of assessing this performance.

Thus the autobiographical is not a space that is open beforehand and in which the grand speculating father tells a story, such and such a story about what has happened to him during his lifetime. Autobiography is *what he tells*. The *fort:da* in question here, as a particular story, is an autobiography that teaches the following: every autobiography is the going out and the coming back of a *fort:da*, e.g., this *fort:da*. But which one? Ernst's? That of his mother, linked with his grandfather in the reading of his own *fort:da*? That of *her* father, in other words, that of his grandfather? The *fort:da* of the father of psychoanalysis? Of the author of *Beyond the Pleasure Principle*? But how can we have access to him without a ghostly analysis[11] of all the others?

How can we say that in recalling what happens to/on the subject (of) Ernst, Freud recalls that this happened to *him*? For several reasons, at least three, which all come down to one.

First: He recalls that Ernst recalls his mother—he recalls Sophie. He recalls that Ernst recalls his daughter in recalling his mother. The ambiguity of the possessive here is not due solely to grammar. Ernst and his grandfather are in a genealogical situation such that the more possessive of the two can always go through the other. Thus the scene immediately opens up the possibility of a permutation of places and of *genitives*, in the strongest sense of the word: the mother of the one is not only the other's mother but also his daughter, and so on and so forth. When the scene was taking place and even before Freud had undertaken to report it, he was already in a position to identify, as we say a bit too readily, with his grandson and, playing it both ways, to recall his mother in recalling his daughter. This privileged identification between grandfather and grandson is frequent, but we shall have more than one proof of this shortly: this identification could be particularly spectacular in the case of the grandfather of psychoanalysis.

I mentioned a second footnote. It was written after the fact and recalls that Sophie is dead: the daughter (mother) recalled by the child died shortly afterward. This supplementary note comes only one page after the first one, but in the meantime, as they say, a page has been turned. Freud has already concluded that the analysis of such an unusual case does not make it possible to come to any sort of firm decision. This conclusion comes after a paragraph full of ins and outs that begins by confirming the rights of the PP: this is the point at which the interpretation of the game explains how the child compensates, indemnifies himself for his suffering (the mother's disappearance) by staging disappearance/reappearance as a game. But Freud immediately dismisses this interpretation insofar as it involves the PP: for if the mother's departure is necessarily unpleasant, how can we explain in terms of the PP the fact that the child reproduces that movement, indeed *more often* in its unpleasant phase (departure, dispatching) than in its pleasant phase (return)? It is at this point that Freud is curiously forced to modify and complete his earlier description. He must say that one phase of the game is more frequently repeated than the other: the completeness of the game is thrown off balance, and Freud hadn't said so before. Most important, he now tells us that the "first act," the departure or *Fortgehen*, was in fact independent: it "was staged as a game in itself." Departure, dispatching, is thus a complete game, practically complete in itself within the entire game. We were right not to accept the earlier allegation of completeness at face value. Because departure is in itself a complete game and is staged more frequently, the explanation by the PP must *fortgehen*, depart in speculative rhetoric. And this is why the analysis of such a case is inconclusive.

But Freud, after this paragraph, does not simply relinquish the PP. He tries it two more times before the final resigned suspension at the end of the chapter.

1. He tries to see in the fact that the child assumes a situation of passivity (not being able to alter his mother's movements) a satisfaction (and thus a pleasure), but the satisfaction of a "drive for mastery" (*Bemächtigungstrieb*), about which Freud suggests oddly that it is "independent" of whether the memory is pleasant or not. It would thus herald something beyond the

PP. But why would such a drive (which appears in other texts by Freud but plays a strangely subdued role here) be foreign to the PP? Why should it not blend into a PP that is often referred to, at least metaphorically, in terms of mastery (*Herrschaft*)? What is the difference between a principle and a drive?

2. After this attempt, Freud tries yet "another interpretation," another recourse to the PP. It involves seeing it as functioning *negatively*. The child might supposedly take pleasure in making the object disappear: throwing the object far away would be satisfying because of his (secondary) interest in its disappearance.

But before I discuss this passage about the two negative workings of the PP, along with the second footnote, I want to extract from the previous paragraph a remark that I have detached only because it seemed to me detachable, like a parasite, from its immediate context. It is perhaps better to read it as an epigraph to what will follow. In the previous paragraph, it has the resonance of a noise from somewhere else, not called for by anything in the previous sentence and not developed by anything in the following one: a sort of loud assertion giving a peremptory answer to an inaudible question. It reads as follows: "It is naturally indifferent from the point of view of the affective evaluation of this game whether the child invented it himself or appropriated it on some outside instigation" (p. 9, translation modified). "Naturally indifferent"? How so? What is an "instigation" in this case? How is it transmitted, and where would it have come from? Would it be so naturally indifferent whether the child had "appropriated" the desire of another, male or female, or of two others who were linked, or whether, inversely, he had occasioned the appropriation of his own game (for it can henceforth happen either way, since the hypothesis is not excluded)? And even if this were true for the "affective evaluation" of the game, which would remain the same in each case, would it be the same for the subject or subjects who would be touched by the affect? All these questions have been put off, dispatched, detached.

I shall now translate Freud's attempt at another interpretation, the section on the negative value of the PP. The successive dispatching of mother and father is pleasurable in this interpretation and calls for a supplementary note.

> But still another interpretation may be attempted. Throwing away the object so that it was "gone" might satisfy an impulse of the child's, which was repressed in his actual life, to revenge himself on his mother for going away from him. In that case it would have a defiant meaning: "All right, then, go away! I don't need you. I'm sending you away myself." A year later, the same boy whom I had observed at his first game used to take a toy, if he was angry with it, and throw it on the floor, exclaiming: "Go to the fwont!" He had heard at that time that his absent father was "at the front," and was far from regretting his absence; on the contrary he gave the clearest indications that he had no desire to be disturbed in his sole possession of his mother. [P. 10, translation modified]

This is where the footnote about Sophie's death appears. Before we get to that, I would stress the assurance with which Freud differentiates the negativity, if that's the word, of the two acts of throwing away. In each case, the daughter (mother) is desired. In the first case the satisfaction of throwing the object away is secondary (revenge, spite); in the second, it is primary. Saying "Stay where you are, and the longer the better" means (according to the PP) "I would have preferred that you return" in the case of the mother and "I prefer that you not return" in the case of the father. This is at least the way his grandfather reads it, the way he reads indications that, he says, are not deceiving: "the clearest indications."

Not deceiving, in any case, about a daughter (mother) who should stay where she is, daughter, mother—a wife, perhaps, but undividedly so, or divided between the two Freuds, in their "sole possession," between her father and her offspring at the moment when her son removes the parasite of his name, the name of the father as the name of the son-in-law.

This is also borne out by Ernst's other brother, his rival, who was born in the meantime, shortly before the daughter (mother) died. Here, at last, is the second note, the supplementary note written after the fact (and the date of its inscription will be important to us):

> When this child was five and three-quarters, his mother died. Now that she was really "gone" [*fort*] ("o-o-o"), the little boy showed no signs of grief. It is true that in the interval a second child had been born and had roused him to violent jealousy. [P. 10, n. 1]

This falling-off would suggest that a dead woman is easier to keep for oneself: one's jealousy is relaxed and idealization interiorizes the object out of the rival's grasp. Thus Sophie, daughter and mother, is dead, preserved from *and* surrendered to each "sole possession." Freud can have the desire to recall (her) and to do all the work of mourning that is necessary.

In the manner of the most heavy-handed psychobiography, some have not failed to connect the problematic of the death drive to Sophie's death. One of their objectives was to reduce the psychoanalytic importance of this "speculation" to that of an episode of reaction. Freud had foreseen this suspicion, and his haste to ward it off is hardly the thing to persuade us that it is unfounded. It is in no way my intention, however, to credit this sort of empiricobiographical explanation, even as a hypothesis. The connection that we are after is a different one, a passage that belongs to a different labyrinth and a different crypt. Still, we must begin by recognizing that Freud himself admits that the hypothesis of such a connection between the death drive and Sophie's death is not senseless, by the very fact that he anticipates it in order to defend against it. This very anticipation and defense are significant for us, and we begin our investigation there.

On 18 December 1923, Freud wrote to Fritz Wittels, author of a book entitled *Sigmund Freud: His Personality, His Teaching, and His School:*[12]

> I certainly would have stressed the connection between the death of the daughter and the concepts of *Beyond* [literally, also "the concepts of the hereafter"] in any analytic study on someone else. Yet still it is wrong. *Beyond the Pleasure Principle* was written in 1919, when my daughter was young and blooming. . . . Probability is not always truth.[13]

Thus Freud admits *probability*. But what *truth* might be involved here? Where is the truth when we are talking about the elaboration of a *fort:da* from which everything is derived, even the concept of truth?

I shall merely "relate" Freud's work after Sophie's definitive *Fortgehen* to the work of his grandson as related in *Beyond the Pleasure Principle*:

1. The irreparable wound *as* a narcissistic insult: all the letters of the period reveal "the feeling of a deep, irreparable blow [*Kränkung*, "insult"] to my narcissism" (to Sándor Ferenczi, 4 February 1920, not two weeks after Sophie's death).[14]

2. But once she is *fort*, Sophie can stay where she is. Her death is "a loss to be forgotten" (to Ernest Jones, 8 February 1920).[15] She is dead, "as if she had never existed" (to Oscar Pfister, 27 January 1920, less than a week after Sophie's death).[16] Thus work goes on, *"geht fort." La séance continue.* This is literally what Freud wrote to Ferenczi to inform him of his bereavement: "My wife is quite overwhelmed. I think: *La séance continue.* But it was a little much for one week" (29 January 1920).[17] This was the same week as the death of Anton von Freund, and we know, at least from the story of the ring,[18] how deep a wound *it* was in what I shall call the Freudian alliance [*alliance*, also "marriage," "wedding band"].

3. The third "related" characteristic is ambivalence about the father—about Ernst's father, that is—the grandfather's son-in-law and Sophie's husband. The struggle for "sole possession" of the dead daughter (mother) breaks out in every quarter, and two days after her decease (*dē* + *cēdere: Fortgehen*), Freud wrote to Pfister:

Sophie leaves behind two boys, one aged six and the other thirteen
months [the one Ernst was jealous of, as he was of his father], and an
inconsolable husband who will now have to pay dearly for the happiness of these seven years. . . . I do as much work as I can and I am grate-
ful for the distraction. The loss of a child seems to be a grave blow to
one's narcissism; as for mourning, that will probably come only later.
[27 January 1920] [19]

The work of mourning will doubtless come only later, but the
work on *Beyond the Pleasure Principle* was not interrupted for
a single day. This letter was written after Sophie's death but
before her cremation. If his work provides "distraction," it's
because he's not working on just anything. (This interval between
the death and the cremation is marked by a story of trains,
indeed of children's trains, the account of which is found in all
of Freud's letters of this week.)[20]

FOREIGN RELATIONS

Classically, the establishment of a science (like psychoanalysis)
should have been able to do without the family name Freud. Or
able, at least, to make forgetting that name the necessary condition and the proof that that science is itself handed on, passed
down. This is what Freud believed or pretended to believe, half
believed, as he half believed in the classic model of science,
the model that he never gave up. Two weeks after Sophie's
death, Freud wrote to Jones. Havelock Ellis had published a
paper maintaining that Freud was a great artist, not a scientist.
Freud, in his response, used the same categories, the same oppo-
sitions, that we are examining here. What the great speculator
is saying is that he is ready to pay for the science [of psycho-
analysis] with his own name [*payer la science de son propre
nom*], to pay the insurance premium with his name. What Ellis
says "is all wrong. I am sure that in a few decades my name will
be wiped away and our results will last" (12 February 1920).[21]
(Note that he can say "we," "our results," and sign all alone.) It

is as if he didn't already know that in paying for the science with his own name, he was also paying for the science *of* his own name, that he was paying (for) himself with a postal money order sent to himself. All that is necessary (!) for this to work is to set up the necessary postal relay system. The science of his own name: a science that for once is essentially inseparable as a science from something like a proper name, a proper-name effect that it claims to account for by accounting *to* that name. But the science of his own name is also what remains to be done, as the necessary return to the origin and the necessary condition for such a science. Now, the speculation we have been discussing may turn out to have consisted in pretending to prepay the charges—whatever the cost—for such a return-to-sender. The calculation is *sans fond* ["bottomless," "has no foundation"; *sans fonds*: "without capital"], and abysslike devaluation or surplus value brings about the ruin even of its very structure. And yet there must be a way to link one's name, the name of one's loved ones (for that's not something you can do alone), to this ruin—a way to speculate on the ruin of one's name that keeps what it loses.

4. Let us continue to analyze the "related" structure of the *Fortgehen*. In the *fort:da*, identification in every sense comes about by way of a structural identification with Ernst. This privileged identification will be paid for once more with an event that is exemplary in more ways than one. It involves Ernst's little brother, the very one who is said to have aroused the jealousy (like another son-in-law) of the older brother, a jealousy that the grandfather can fully understand.

In 1923 the fatal malignancy of Freud's cancer of the mouth was revealed, and he had the first of thirty-three operations. As early as 1918, he had thought he was going to die, but then recalled his mother:

> My mother will be eighty-three this year, and is now rather shaky. Sometimes I think I shall feel a little freer when she dies, because the

> idea of her having to be told of my death is something from which one
> shrinks back. [to Karl Abraham, 29 May 1918][22]

Every speculation, as we said earlier, implies the frightening possibility of this *hysteron proteron* of the generations. (Freud himself wrote after Sophie's death that neither he nor his wife had "got over the monstrous fact of children dying before their parents" [to Ludwig Binswanger, 14 March 1920].)[23] The return of the figureless figure, the nameless name of the mother, when all is done and accounted for, is what I call in *Glas* "obsequent logic"; the mother buries her own, all of them, and she follows all the funeral processions.

We said that the first operation on his mouth was in 1923. "His," i.e., the grandfather's, but also Heinerle's, Sophie's second son (Heinz Rudolf), Ernst's younger brother—a tonsillectomy. Heinerle was Freud's favorite grandson, the favorite son of his favorite daughter, the boy Freud called "the most intelligent child he had ever encountered."[24] They spoke together about their two operations as if they were one.

After the operation, further weakened by miliary tuberculosis and less resistant than his grandfather, Heinerle died. On 19 June 1923 Freud was seen crying, the only time in his life. In 1926 Freud told Binswanger what Heinerle had meant to him: Heinerle had stood for all his children and grandchildren. Thus, he saw in Heinerle's death the death of all his progeny: "It is the secret of my indifference—people call it courage—toward the danger to my own life" (to Binswanger, 15 October 1926).[25]

On 2 November 1925 he also confided in Marie Bonaparte: since the death of the boy who had stood for all his progeny, as sole legatee and affectively the bearer of the name (the descent of the community being insured by the woman, in this case the "favorite" daughter, and the second grandson is to bear the name of his maternal grandfather—this could all be determined by Judaic law)—since Heinerle's death, he had been unable to form any new attachments and could only keep up the old ones.[26] No more ties, no more contracts, no more alliances, no more vows that might attach him to some future, to some posterity. And when the ties are all to the past, they are past. But Marie Bonaparte, who was part of the old alliance, received the confidence, the certification of this confidence that in some way renews involvement by declaring it past. She was to hold in trust this certification of inheritance. If I stress this avowal to Marie Bonaparte, it is because I wish to do some forwarding by way of the purveyor of truth[27] to the family scene on the French side, at the moment that the seal is broken, supposedly, on a will. Who then will not *enter* into "sole possession" (as we say "to join the fray" or "to go into a panic")? One of the elements in the drama is that several families have the same name without always knowing it. And there are other names in the same family.

In 1923, Heinerle is gone (*fort*), but the pains in Freud's mouth remain, terrible and threatening. He is more than half sure what they hold in store for him. He wrote to Felix Deutsch: "A comprehensible indifference to most of the trivialities of life shows me that the work of mourning is going on in the depths. Among these trivialities I count science itself" (8 August 1923).[28] As if the name should really be forgotten, and this time *along with* the science. But even if he more than half believed it, this time or the last, when he tied the science to the loss of the name, would *we* believe it? No more this time than the last.

If we seek to understand the closure of the Freudian alliance to the future, we must perhaps draw other threads from the past. Let us mention Julius, Freud's little brother, who was to Freud as Heinerle was to Ernst. Julius died at the age of eight months; Freud was then the same age that Ernst was at the time that the *fort:da* was observed, one and a half. Ernest Jones writes:

Before the newcomer's birth the infant Freud had had sole access to his mother's love and milk, and he had to learn from the experience how strong the jealousy of a young child can be. In a letter to Fliess (1897) he admits the evil wishes he had against his rival and adds that their fulfillment in his death had aroused self-reproaches, a tendency which had remained ever since.[29]

How can we separate this graph from that of the legacy? Yet between the two, there is no causal connection, nor is one a condition for the possibility of the other. Repetition is bequeathed; the legacy is repeated.

If Freud's guilt is related back to the person whose death Freud experienced as his own, *that is*, that of the other (the death of Ernst's younger brother as the death of his younger brother, Julius), then we have some (and only some) of the threads, some of the strings in the snare of murderous, bereaved, jealous, infinitely guilty identifications, that catches speculation in its trap. But as the snare constrains speculation, it also constrains *to* speculation with its rigorous stricture. The legacy and the jealousy of a repetition (already jealous of itself) are not accidents that just happen to the *fort:da*: they pull its strings, more or less strictly. And they assign it to an auto-bio-thanato-hetero-graphic writing scene.

NOTES

"Coming into One's Own," which treats a portion of the second chapter of Freud's *Beyond the Pleasure Principle*, is three steps removed from being "a text by Jacques Derrida." It is part of a much longer work in progress (as yet untitled) that studies *Beyond the Pleasure Principle* chapter by chapter, often line by line. Because of limitations of space, this section has been abridged by more than one third: cuts have been made in almost every paragraph, and many paragraphs have been omitted entirely. Finally, it is a translation of a writer and thinker whose work exploits the resources of language and languages at every turn. I have made the cuts, occasionally juggled sentences, divided the text into sections, and supplied all the titles, as part of this effort of translation. All notes are translator's notes, unless otherwise indicated.

Two sets of expressions require some preliminary clarification. The words "speculator," "speculation," and "speculative" recur both here and in *Beyond the Pleasure Principle*; Derrida has said that this speculating, for Freud a method of research, is the object of his (Derrida's) discourse in the text from which "Coming into One's

Own" is taken. The reader should remember all of the lexical (including that of financial speculation) and etymological (including "observer" and "mirror") associations of these words.

"PP" and "PR" are the initials of the French expressions for "pleasure principle" and "reality principle," respectively, concepts developed early in *Beyond the Pleasure Principle* and Derrida's text. At the same time, the French pronunciations of these initials sound like the equivalents of "granddaddy" (*pépé*) and "father" (*père*). (This homonymy links the authority of the pleasure principle and that of the grandfather or grandfathers evoked in the text.) When these initials appear in the text, it is necessary to preserve (and read) both meanings; this is the reason for awkward constructions like "it/he" when the antecedent is "PP"—a problem that exists only when the text is translated.—J. H.

Quotations not otherwise identified are from *Beyond the Pleasure Principle*, trans. James Strachey (New York: Norton, n.d.); the translation has been modified as necessary. The bibliography suggested by Derrida from his own writings includes "Freud and the Scene of Writing," *Yale French Studies*, no. 48 (1972), pp. 73-117; *Glas* (Paris: Galilée, 1974); "The Purveyor of Truth," *Yale French Studies*, no. 52 (1975), pp. 31-113; and "Fors," *Georgia Review* 31 (1977): 64-116. The most useful guide to psychoanalytic terminology is Jean Laplanche and J.-B. Pontalis, *The Language of Psycho-analysis* (New York: Norton, 1973).

1. The word *fil* is translated as "string," "wire," or "thread," depending on the context; its plural, *fils*, is written in the same way as the words for "son" and "sons."

2. Derrida notes in an earlier section that if nothing has contradicted the authority of the PP, it is "perhaps because the PP cannot be contradicted. . . . From the moment there is speech, the absolute master is confirmed, the PP that as such cannot be silent." However, "on the last page of *Beyond the Pleasure Principle*, it is said that the death drives say nothing. They 'seem to do their work unobtrusively,' subjugating to their service the master himself, who continues to speak loudly: the PP."

3. The family relations are as follows: Freud had three daughters, Mathilde, Sophie, and Anna; Sophie's sons, Ernst and Heinerle, are referred to in *Beyond the Pleasure Principle*, but never by name and never as Freud's grandchildren.

4. *Les siens*: "his," "the members of his family," "his own," "his loved ones." The expression occurs frequently in the text, linking one's own (self) to one's own family: among other things, one is one of one's own.

5. This refers to a frequent notion in Hegel, most simply expressed in the introduction to the *Science of Logic* [i.e., the "Greater Logic"], trans. A. V. Miller (London: Allen & Unwin, 1969), p. 56: "It is in . . . the grasping of opposites in their unity . . . that speculative thought consists." See also Hegel's introduction to his *Lectures on the Philosophy of Religion*, trans. E. B. Speirs and J. B. Sanderson, 3 vols. (1895; reprint ed., New York: The Humanities Press, 1962), 1:21-22.

6. Je vous laisse suivre ce facteur: "*facteur*," which also means "mailman," suggests the Derrida text entitled "Le Facteur de la vérité," translated as "The Purveyor of Truth."

7. The expression "*mise en abyme*," originally from heraldry, where it denotes a smaller escutcheon appearing in the center of a larger one, is now frequent in literary discussions, as popularized by Gide (*Journal, 1889-1939* [Paris: Bibliothèque de la Pléiade, n.d.], p. 41), to refer to a structure in which the whole is represented in

miniature in one of its parts. An example would be a painting of a drawing room in which a painting hung, also of a drawing room, ideally the same drawing room, complete with painting, etc. The most famous literary example is Gide's *Counterfeiters*. "*Abyme*" is an old spelling for "*abîme*," "abyss" (etymologically, "bottomless"). The *abyme* structure is usually said to be dizzying, unsettling.

8. The German word "*Spielzeug*" can refer either to a single toy or, as a collective noun (and in Freud's sentence), to a child's playthings. The element "*-zeug*" (stuff, material, equipment, tools) is important because of its valorization by Heidegger, using the latter senses. See the section of "The Origin of the Work of Art" entitled "Thing and Work," in Martin Heidegger, *Poetry, Language, Thought* (New York: Harper & Row, 1971), esp. pp. 29-39.

9. Derrida stresses that *Beyond the Pleasure Principle* is a text without a thesis; it establishes nothing, there is no bedrock, and it is never proved or decided that there is anything "beyond the pleasure principle." If we seek *la thèse* of *Beyond the Pleasure Principle*, we find *l'athèse* of *Beyond the Pleasure Principle*. (Cf. "*athée*," "*athéisme*.")

10. On the double stricture of the *lacet* as it relates to the *fort:da*, see Derrida, *Glas*, and "Restitutions," in *La Vérité en peinture* (Paris: Flammarion, 1978).—J.D.

11. *Analyse spectrale*, also the technical expression for "spectrum analysis."

12. (New York: Dodd, Mead, 1924)

13. Ernest Jones, *The Life and Works of Sigmund Freud*, 3 vols. (New York: Basic Books, 1953-57), 3: 40-41, translation modified.

14. Ibid., 3: 20, translation modified.

15. Max Schur, *Freud: Living and Dying* (New York: International Universities Press, 1972), p. 330.

16. Jones, *Sigmund Freud*, 3: 19, translation modified.

17. Ibid., 3: 19.

18. "Necessary insignia" of membership in the "Committee." Von Freund, aware that he was dying, "ordered the ring Freud had given him to be restored after his death so that it could be passed over to Eitingon. Von Freund was to have been a member of the private 'Committee,' but Eitingon took his place. After von Freund's death, however, his widow claimed the ring, so Freud gave Eitingon the one he had himself worn" (ibid., 3: 18-19). On the "Committee" and its rings, see ibid., 2: 151-67, esp. 154; for the juxtaposition of the germ of the Committee, Sophie's engagement and Freud's future son-in-law, and Lear's/Freud's three daughters, see ibid., 2: 93.

19. Schur, *Freud*, p. 330, translation modified.

20. Derrida's complete text here reproduces parts of two of Freud's letters: to Binswanger, 14 March 1920, and to Pfister, 27 January 1920 (ibid., pp. 329-30).

21. Jones, *Sigmund Freud*, 3: 21.

22. Schur, *Freud*, pp. 314-15.

23. Ibid., p. 329.

24. Jones, *Sigmund Freud*, 3: 91.

25. Ibid., 3:92.

26. Ibid.

27. See note 6 above and Derrida, "Purveyor of Truth," esp. pp. 66-71.

28. Jones, *Sigmund Freud*, 3: 91, translation modified.

29. Ibid., 1: 7-8.

Barbara Johnson

The Frame of Reference:
Poe, Lacan, Derrida

A literary text that both analyzes itself and shows that it actually has neither a self nor any neutral metalanguage with which to do the analyzing calls out irresistibly for analysis. And when that call is answered by two eminent thinkers whose readings emit an equally paradoxical call to analysis of their own, the resulting triptych, in the context of the question of the act of reading (literature), places *its* would-be reader in a vertiginously insecure position.

The three texts in question are Edgar Allan Poe's short story "The Purloined Letter,"[1] Jacques Lacan's "Seminar on The Purloined Letter,"[2] and Jacques Derrida's reading of Lacan's reading of Poe, "The Purveyor of Truth" (Le Facteur de la Vérité).[3] In all three texts, it is the *act of analysis* that seems to occupy the center of the discursive stage and the *act of analysis of the act of analysis* that in some way disrupts that centrality, subverting the very possibility of a position of analytical mastery. In the resulting asymmetrical, abysmal structure, no analysis—including this one—can intervene without transforming and repeating other elements in the sequence, which is thus not a stable sequence, but which nevertheless produces certain regular effects. It is the functioning of this regularity, and the structure of these effects, that will provide the basis for the present study.

Any attempt to do "justice" to three such complex texts is obviously out of the question. But it is precisely the *nature* of such "justice" that *is* the question in each of these readings of the act of analysis. The fact that the debate proliferates around a crime story—a robbery and its undoing—can hardly be an accident. Somewhere in each of these texts, the economy of justice cannot be avoided. For in spite of the absence of mastery, there is no lack of *effects of power*.

I shall begin by quoting at some length from Lacan's discussion of "The Purloined Letter" in order to present both the plot of Poe's story and the thrust of Lacan's analysis. Lacan summarizes the story as follows:

> There are two scenes, the first of which we shall straightway designate the primal scene, and by no means inadvertently, since the second may be considered its repetition in the very sense we are considering today. The primal scene is thus performed, we are told, in the royal *boudoir*, so that we suspect that the person of the highest rank, called the "exalted personage", who is alone there when she receives a letter, is the Queen. This feeling is confirmed by the embarrassment into which she is plunged by the entry of the other exalted personage, of whom we have already been told prior to this account that the knowledge he might have of the letter in question would jeopardize for the lady nothing less than her honor and safety. Any doubt that he is in fact the King is promptly dissipated in the course of the scene which begins with the entry of the Minister D. . . . At that moment, in fact, the Queen can do no better than to play on the King's inattentiveness by leaving the letter on the table "face down, address uppermost." It does not, however, escape the Minister's lynx eye, nor does he fail to notice the Queen's distress and thus to fathom her secret. From then on everything transpires like clockwork. After dealing in his customary manner with the business of the day, the Minister draws from his pocket a letter similar in appearance to the one in his view, and, having pretended to read it, places it next to the other. A bit more conversation to amuse the royal company, whereupon, without flinching once, he seizes the embarrassing letter, making off with it, as the Queen, on whom none of his maneuver has been lost, remains unable to intervene for fear of attracting the attention of her royal spouse, close at her side at that very moment.
>
> Everything might then have transpired unseen by a hypothetical spectator of an operation in which nobody falters, and whose *quotient* is that the Minister has filched from the Queen her letter and that—an even more important result than the first—the Queen knows that he now has it, and by no means innocently.
>
> A *remainder* that no analyst will neglect, trained as he is to retain

whatever is significant, without always knowing what to do with it: the letter, abandoned by the Minister, and which the Queen's hand is now free to roll into a ball.

Second scene: in the Minister's office. It is in his hotel, and we know—from the account the Prefect of Police has given Dupin, whose specific genius for solving enigmas Poe introduces here for the second time—that the police, returning there as soon as the Minister's habitual, nightly absences allow them to, have searched the hotel and surroundings from top to bottom for the last eighteen months. In vain—although everyone can deduce from the situation that the Minister keeps the letter within reach.

Dupin calls on the Minister. The latter receives him with studied non-chalance, affecting in his conversation romantic *ennui*. Meanwhile Dupin, whom this pretense does not deceive, his eyes protected by green glasses, proceeds to inspect the premises. When his glance catches a rather crumbled piece of paper—apparently thrust carelessly in a division of an ugly pasteboard card-rack, hanging gaudily from the middle of the mantelpiece—he already knows that he's found what he's looking for. His conviction is reinforced by the very details which seem to contradict the description he has of the stolen letter, with the exception of the format, which remains the same.

Whereupon he has but to withdraw, after "forgetting" his snuffbox on the table, in order to return the following day to reclaim it—armed with a facsimile of the letter in its present state. As an incident in the street, prepared for the proper moment, draws the Minister to the window, Dupin in turn seizes the opportunity to seize the letter while substituting the imitation, and has only to maintain the appearances of a normal exit.

Here as well all has transpired, if not without noise, at least without all commotion. The quotient of the operation is that the Minister no longer has the letter, but, far from suspecting that Dupin is the culprit who has ravished it from him, knows nothing of it. Moreover, what he is left with is far from insignificant for what follows. We shall return to what brought Dupin to inscribe a message on his counterfeit letter. Whatever the case, the Minister, when he tries to make use of it, will be able to read these words, written so that he may recognize Dupin's hand: " . . . Un dessein si funeste/S'il n'est digne d'Atrée est digne de Thyeste,"[4] whose source, Dupin tells us, is Crébillon's *Atrée*.

Need we emphasize the similarity of these two sequences? Yes, for the resemblance we have in mind is not a simple collection of traits chosen only in order to delete their difference. And it would not be enough to retain those common traits at the expense of the others for the slightest truth to result. It is rather the intersubjectivity in which the two actions are motivated that we wish to bring into relief, as well as the three terms through which it structures them.

The special status of these terms results from their corresponding simultaneously to the three logical moments through which the decision is precipitated and the three places it assigns to the subjects among whom it constitutes a choice.

That decision is reached in a glance's time. For the maneuvers which follow, however stealthily they prolong it, add nothing to that glance, nor does the deferring of the deed in the second scene break the unity of that moment.

This glance presupposes two others, which it embraces in its vision of the breach left in their fallacious complementarity, anticipating in it the occasion for larceny afforded by that exposure. Thus three moments, structuring three glances, borne by three subjects, incarnated each time by different characters.

The first is a glance that sees nothing: the King and the police.

The second, a glance which sees that the first sees nothing and deludes itself as to the secrecy of what it hides; the Queen, then the Minister.

The third sees that the first two glances leave what should be hidden exposed to whomever would seize it: the Minister and finally Dupin.

In order to grasp in its unity the intersubjective complex thus described, we would willingly seek a model in the technique legendarily attributed to the ostrich attempting to shield itself from danger; for that technique might ultimately be qualified as political, divided as it here is among three partners: the second believing itself invisible because the first has its head stuck in the ground, and all the while letting the third calmly pluck its rear; we need only enrich its proverbial denomination by a letter, producing *la politique de l'autruiche*,[5] for the ostrich itself to take on forever a new meaning.

Given the intersubjective modulus of the repetitive action, it remains to recognize in it a *repetition automatism* in the sense that interests us in Freud's text. [*SPL*, pp. 41–44]

Thus, it is neither the character of the individual subjects, nor the contents of the letter, but the *position* of the letter within the group that decides what each person will do next. It is the fact that the letter does *not* function as a unit of meaning (a signified) but as that which produces certain effects (a signifier) that leads Lacan to read the story as an illustration of "the truth which may be drawn from that moment in Freud's thought under study—namely, that it is the symbolic order which is constitutive for the subject—by demonstrating . . . the decisive orientation which the subject receives from the itinerary of a signifier" [*SPL*, p. 40]. The letter acts like a signifier precisely to the extent that its function in the story does not require that its meaning be revealed: "the letter was able to produce its effects *within* the story: on the actors in the tale, including the narrator, as well as *outside* the story: on us, the readers, and also on its author, without anyone's ever bothering to worry about what it *meant*."[6] "The Purloined Letter" thus becomes for Lacan a kind of *allegory of the signifier*.

Derrida's critique of Lacan's reading does not dispute the validity of the allegorical interpretation on its own terms, but questions rather its implicit presuppositions and its modus operandi. Derrida aims his objections at two kinds of targets: (1) what Lacan *puts into* the letter, and (2) what Lacan *leaves out of* the text.

(1) *What Lacan puts into the letter.* While asserting that the letter's meaning is lacking, Lacan, according to Derrida, makes this lack into *the* meaning of the letter. But Derrida does not stop there: he goes on to assert that what Lacan means by that lack is the truth of lack-as-castration-as-truth: "The truth of the purloined letter is the truth itself. . . . What is veiled/unveiled in this case is a hole, a nonbeing [*non-étant*]; the truth of being [*l'être*], as nonbeing. Truth is "woman" as veiled/unveiled castration" [*PT*, pp. 60-61]. Lacan himself, however, never uses the word "castration" in the text of the original seminar. That it is suggested is indisputable, but Derrida, by filling in what *Lacan* left blank, is repeating precisely the gesture of blank-filling for which he is criticizing Lacan.

(2) *What Lacan leaves out of the text*. This objection is itself double: on the one hand, Derrida criticizes Lacan for neglecting to consider "The Purloined Letter" in connection with the other two stories in what Derrida calls Poe's "Dupin Trilogy." And on the other hand, according to Derrida, at the very moment Lacan is reading the story as an allegory of the signifier, he is being blind to the disseminating power of the signifier in the *text* of the allegory, in what Derrida calls the "scene of writing." To cut out part of a text's frame of reference as though it did not exist and to reduce a complex textual functioning to a single meaning are serious blots indeed in the annals of literary criticism. Therefore it is all the more noticeable that Derrida's own reading of Lacan's text repeats precisely the crimes of which he accuses it: on the one hand, Derrida makes no mention of Lacan's long development on the relation between symbolic determination and random series. And on the other hand, Derrida dismisses Lacan's "style" as a mere ornament, veiling, for a time, an unequivocal message: "Lacan's 'style', moreover, was such that for a long time it would hinder and delay all access to a *unique* content or a single unequivocal meaning determinable beyond the writing itself" [*PT*, p. 40]. The fact that Derrida repeats the very gestures he is criticizing does not in itself invalidate his criticism of their *effects*, but it does render problematic his statement condemning their *existence*. And it also illustrates the transfer of the repetition compulsion from the original *text* to the scene of its *reading*.

In an attempt to read this paradoxical encounter more closely, let us examine the way in which Derrida deduces from Lacan's text the fact that, for Lacan, the "letter" is a symbol of the (mother's) phallus. Since Lacan never uses the word "phallus" in the seminar, this is already an *interpretation* on Derrida's part, and quite an astute one at that. Lacan, as a later reader of his own seminar, implicitly agrees with it by placing the word "castrated"—which had not been used in the original text—in his "Points" presentation. The disagreement between Derrida and Lacan thus arises not over the *validity* of the equation "letter=phallus," but over its *meaning*.

How, then, does Derrida derive this equation from Lacan's text? The deduction follows four basic lines of reasoning:

1. The letter "belongs" to the Queen as a substitute for the phallus she does not have. It feminizes (castrates) each of its successive holders and is eventually returned to her as its rightful owner.

2. Poe's description of the position of the letter in the Minister's apartment, expanded upon by the figurative dimensions of Lacan's text, suggests an analogy between the shape of the fireplace, from the center of whose mantelpiece the letter is found hanging, and that point on a woman's anatomy from which the phallus is missing.

3. The letter, says Lacan, cannot be divided: "But if it is first of all on the materiality of the signifier that we have insisted, that materiality is *odd* [singulière] in many ways, the first of which is not to admit partition" [*SPL*, p. 53]. This indivisibility, says Derrida, is odd indeed, but becomes comprehensible if it is seen as an *idealization* of the phallus, whose integrity is necessary for the edification of the entire psychoanalytical system. With the phallus safely idealized the so-called "signifier" acquires the "unique, living, non-mutilable integrity" of the self-present spoken word, unequivocally pinned down to and by the *signified*. "Had the phallus been per(mal)chance divisible or reduced to the status of a partial object, the whole edification would have crumbled down, and this is what has to be avoided at all cost" [*PT*, pp. 96–97].

4. Finally, if Poe's story "illustrates" the "truth," as Lacan puts it, the last words of the seminar proper seem to reaffirm that truth in no uncertain terms: "Thus it is that what the 'purloined letter' . . . means is that *a letter always arrives at its destination*" [*SPL*, p. 72, emphasis mine]. Now, since it is unlikely that Lacan

is talking about the efficiency of the postal service, he must, according to Derrida, be affirming the possibility of unequivocal meaning, the eventual reappropriation of the message, its total equivalence with itself. And since the "truth" Poe's story illustrates is, in Derrida's eyes, the truth of veiled/unveiled castration and of the transcendental identity of the phallus as the lack that makes the system work, this final sentence in Lacan's seminar seems to affirm both the absolute truth of psychoanalytical theories and the absolute decipherability of the literary text. Poe's message will have been totally, unequivocally understood and explained by the psychoanalytical myth. "The hermeneutic discovery of meaning (truth), the deciphering (that of Dupin and that of the seminar), arrives itself at its destination" [*PT*, p. 66].

Thus, the law of the phallus seems to imply a reappropriating return to the place of true ownership, an indivisible identity functioning beyond the possibility of disintegration or unrecoverable loss, and a totally self-present, unequivocal meaning or truth. The problem with this type of system, counters Derrida, is that it cannot account for the possibility of sheer accident, irreversible loss, unreappropriable residues, and infinite divisibility, which are in fact necessary and inevitable in the system's very elaboration. In order for the circuit of the letter to end up confirming the law of the phallus, it must begin by transgressing it: the letter is a sign of high treason. Phallogocentrism mercilessly represses the uncontrollable multiplicity of ambiguities, the disseminating play of *writing*, which irreducibly transgresses any unequivocal meaning. "Not that the letter never arrives at its destination, but part of its structure is that it is always capable of not arriving there. . . . Here dissemination threatens the law of the signifier and of castration as a contract of truth. Dissemination mutilates the unity of the signifier, that is, of the phallus" [*PT*, p. 66]. In contrast to Lacan's *Seminar*, then, Derrida's text would seem to be setting itself up as a *Disseminar*.

From the foregoing remarks, it can easily be seen that the disseminal criticism of Lacan's apparent reduction of the literary text to an unequivocal message depends for its force upon the presupposition of unambiguousness in *Lacan's* text. And indeed, the statement that a letter always reaches its destination seems straightforward enough. But when that statement is reinserted into its context, things become palpably less certain:

> Is that all, and shall we believe we have deciphered Dupin's real strategy above and beyond the imaginary tricks with which he was obliged to deceive us? No doubt, yes, for if "any point requiring reflection", as Dupin states at the start, is "examined to best purpose in the dark", we may now easily read its solution in broad daylight. It was already implicit and easy to derive from the title of our tale, according to the very formula we have long submitted to your discretion: in which the sender, we tell you, receives from the receiver his own message in reverse form. Thus it is that what the "purloined letter," nay, the "letter in sufferance" means is that a letter always arrives at its destination. [*SPL*, p. 72]

The meaning of this last sentence is problematized not so much by its own ambiguity as by a series of reversals in the preceding sentences. If the best examination takes place in darkness, what does "reading in broad daylight" imply? Could it not be taken as an affirmation not of actual lucidity but of *delusions* of lucidity? Could it not then move the "yes, no doubt" as an answer not to the question "have we deciphered?" but to the question "shall we *believe* we have deciphered?" And if this is possible, does it not empty the final affirmation of all unequivocality, leaving it to stand with the *force* of an assertion, without any definite content? And if the sender receives from the receiver his own message backwards, who is the sender here, who is the receiver, and what is the message? I will take another look at this passage later, but for the moment its ambiguities seem sufficient to problematize, if not subvert, the presupposition of univocality that is the very foundation on which Derrida has edified his interpretation.

Surely such an oversimplification on Derrida's part does not
result from mere blindness, oversight, or error. As Paul de Man
says of Derrida's similar treatment of Rousseau, "the pattern is
too interesting not to be deliberate."[7] Derrida's consistent
forcing of Lacan's statements into systems and patterns from
which they are actually trying to escape must correspond to
some strategic necessity different from the attentiveness to the
letter of the text that characterizes Derrida's way of reading
Poe. And in fact, the more one works with Derrida's analysis,
the more convinced one becomes that although the critique of
what Derrida *calls* psychoanalysis is entirely justified, it does
not quite apply to what Lacan's text is actually saying. What
Derrida is in fact arguing against is therefore not Lacan's text
but Lacan's power, or rather, "Lacan" as the apparent cause of
certain *effects of power* in French discourse today. Whatever
Lacan's text may *say*, it *functions*, according to Derrida, as if
it said what *he* says it says. The statement that a letter always
reaches its destination may be totally undecipherable, but its
assertive force is taken all the more seriously as a sign that
Lacan himself has everything all figured out. Such an assertion,
in fact, gives him an appearance of mastery like that of the
Minister in the eyes of the letterless Queen. "The ascendancy
which the Minister derives from the situation," explains Lacan,
"is attached not to the letter but to the character it makes him
into."

Thus Derrida's seemingly "blind" reading, whose vagaries we
are following here, is not a mistake, but the positioning of what
can be called the "average reading" of Lacan's text, which is the
true object of Derrida's deconstruction. Since Lacan's text is
read as if it said what Derrida says it says, its actual textual
functioning is irrelevant to the agonistic arena in which Derrida's
analysis takes place. If Derrida's reading of Lacan's reading of
Poe is thus actually the deconstruction of a reading whose
status is difficult to determine, does this mean that Lacan's text

is completely innocent of the misdemeanors of which it is accused? If Lacan can be shown to be opposed to the same kind of logocentric error that Derrida is opposed to, does that mean that they are both really saying the same thing? These are questions that must be left, at least for the moment, hanging.

But the structure of Derrida's *transference of guilt* from a certain *reading* of Lacan onto Lacan's *text* is not indifferent in itself, in the context of what, after all, started out as a relatively simple crime story. For what it amounts to is nothing less than—a *frame*. And if Derrida is thus framing Lacan for an interpretative malpractice of which he himself is, at least in part, the author, what can this frame teach us about the nature of the act of reading, in the context of the question of literature and psychoanalysis?

Interestingly enough, one of the major crimes for which Lacan is being framed by Derrida is precisely the psychoanalytical reading's elimination of what Derrida calls the literary text's *frame*. That frame here consists not only of the two stories that precede "The Purloined Letter," but of the stratum of narration through which the stories are told, and, "beyond" it, of the text's entire functioning as *écriture*.

It would seem that Lacan is guilty of several sins of omission: the omission of the narrator, of the nondialogue parts of the story, and of the other stories in the trilogy. But does this criticism amount to a mere plea for the inclusion of what has been excluded? No, the problem is not simply quantitative. What has been excluded is not homogeneous to what has been included. Lacan, says Derrida, misses the specifically literary dimension of Poe's text by treating it as a "real drama," a story like the stories a psychoanalyst hears every day from his patients. What has been left out is precisely *literature* itself.

Does this mean that the "frame" is what makes a text literary? In a recent issue of *New Literary History* devoted to the question "What is Literature?" and totally unrelated to the debate

concerning the purloined letter, this is precisely the conclusion
to which one of the contributors comes: "Literature is language, . . . but it is language around which we have drawn a
frame, a frame that indicates a decision to regard with a particular self-consciousness the resources language has always possessed."[8]

Such a view of literature, however, implies that a text is
literary *because* it remains inside certain definite borders: it is
a many-faceted object, perhaps, but still, it is an object. That
this is not quite what Derrida has in mind becomes clear from
the following remarks:

> By overlooking the narrator's position, the narrator's involvement in
> the content of what he seems to be recounting, one omits from the
> scene of writing anything going beyond the two triangular scenes.
>   And first of all one omits that what is in question—with no possible
> access route or border—is a scene of writing whose boundaries crumble
> off into an abyss. From the simulacrum of an overture, of a "first
> word," the narrator, in narrating himself, advances a few propositions
> that carry the unity of the "tale" into an endless drifting off course: a
> textual drifting not at all taken into account in the seminar. [*PT*, pp.
> 100–101; translation modified]

> These reminders, of which countless other examples could be given,
> alert us to the effects of the frame, and of the paradoxes in the parer-
> gonal logic. Our purpose is not to prove that "The Purloined Letter"
> functions within a frame (omitted by the seminar, which can thus be
> assured of its triangular interior by an active, surreptitious limitation
> starting from a metalinguistic overview), but to prove that the structure
> of the framing effects is such that no totalization of the border is even
> possible. Frames are always framed: thus, by part of their content.
> Pieces without a whole, "divisions" without a totality—this is what
> thwarts the dream of a letter without division, allergic to division.
> [*PT*, p. 99; translation modified]

Here the argument seems to reverse the previous objection:
Lacan has eliminated not the frame but the unframability of
the literary text. But what Derrida calls "parergonal logic" is

paradoxical precisely because *both* of these incompatible (but not totally contradictory) arguments are equally valid. The total inclusion of the "frame" is both mandatory and impossible. The "frame" thus becomes not the borderline between the inside and the outside, but precisely what subverts the applicability of the inside/outside polarity to the act of interpretation.

What enables Derrida to problematize the literary text's frame is, as we have seen, what he calls "the scene of writing." By this he means two things:

1. The textual signifier's resistance to being totally transformed into a signified. In spite of Lacan's attentiveness to the path of the letter in Poe's story as an illustration of the functioning of a signifier, says Derrida, the psychoanalytical reading is still blind to the functioning of the signifier *in the narration itself*. In reading "The Purloined Letter" as an *allegory* of the signifier, Lacan, according to Derrida, has made the "signifier" into the story's truth: "The displacement of the signifier is analyzed as a signified, as the recounted object in a short story" [*PT*, p. 48]. Whereas, counters Derrida, it is precisely the *textual* signifier that resists being thus totalized into meaning, leaving an irreducible residue: "The rest, the remnant, would be 'The Purloined Letter,' the text that bears this title, and whose place, like the once more invisible large letters on the map, is not where one was expecting to find it, in the enclosed content of the 'real drama' or in the hidden and sealed interior of Poe's story, but in and as the open letter, the very open letter which fiction is" [*PT*, p. 64].

2. The actual writings—the books, libraries, quotations, and previous tales—that surround "The Purloined Letter" with a *frame* of (literary) *references*. The story begins in "a little back library, or book-closet" [*Poe*, p. 199] where the narrator is mulling over a previous conversation on the subject of the two previous instances of Dupin's detective work as told in Poe's two previous tales (the first of which recounted the original

meeting between Dupin and the narrator—in a *library*, of course, where both were in search of the same rare book). The story's beginning is thus an infinitely regressing reference to previous writings. And therefore, says Derrida, "nothing begins. Simply a drifting or a disorientation from which one never moves away" [*PT*, p. 101]. Dupin himself is in fact a walking library: books are his "sole luxuries," and the narrator is "astonished" at "the vast extent of his reading" [*Poe*, p. 106]. Even Dupin's last, most seemingly personal words—the venomous lines he leaves in his substitute letter to the Minister—are a quotation; a quotation whose transcription and proper authorship are the last things the story tells us. "But," concludes Derrida, "beyond the quotation marks that surround the entire story, Dupin is obliged to quote this last word in quotation marks, to recount his signature: that is what I wrote to him and how I signed it. What is a signature within quotation marks? Then, within these quotation marks, the seal itself is a quotation within quotation marks. This remnant is still literature" [*PT*, pp. 112-13].

It is by means of these two extra dimensions that Derrida intends to show the crumbling, abysmal, nontotalizable edges of the story's frame. Both of these objections, however, are in themselves more problematic and double-edged than they appear. I shall begin with the second. "Literature," in Derrida's demonstration, is indeed clearly the beginning, middle, and end—and even the interior—of the purloined letter. But how was this conclusion reached? To a large extent, by listing the books, libraries, and other writings *recounted* in the story. That is, by following the *theme*, not the functioning, of "writing" within "the content of a representation." But if the fact that Dupin signs with a quotation, for example, is for Derrida a sign that "this remnant is still literature," does this not indicate that "literature" has become not the signifier but the *signified* in the story? If the play of the signifier is really to be followed, doesn't it play beyond the range of the *seme* "writing?" And if

Derrida criticizes Lacan for making the "signifier" into the story's "signified," is Derrida not here transforming "writing" into "the written" in much the same way? What Derrida calls "the reconstruction of the scene of the signifier as a signified" seems indeed to be "an inevitable process" in the logic of reading the purloined letter.

Derrida, of course, implicitly counters this objection by protesting—twice—that the textual drifting for which Lacan does not account should not be considered "the *real subject* of the tale," but rather the "remarkable ellipsis" of any subject. But the question of the seemingly inevitable slipping from the signifier to the signified still remains. And it remains not as an *objection* to the logic of the frame, but as its fundamental *question*. For if the "paradoxes of parergonal logic" are such that the frame is always being framed by part of its contents, it is precisely this slippage between signifier and signified (which is *acted out* by both Derrida and Lacan against their intentions) that best illustrates those paradoxes. If the question of the frame thus problematizes the object of any interpretation by setting it at an angle or fold with itself, then Derrida's analysis errs not in opposing this paradoxical functioning to Lacan's allegorical reading, but in not following the consequences of its own insight far enough.

Another major point in Derrida's critique is that psychoanalysis, wherever it looks, is capable of finding only itself. The first sentence of *The Purveyor of Truth* is: "Psychoanalysis, supposing, finds itself" ["La psychanalyse, à supposer, se trouve"]. In whatever it turns its attention to, psychoanalysis seems to recognize nothing but its own (Oedipal) schemes. Dupin finds the letter because "he knows that the letter finally *finds itself* where it must *be found* in order to return circularly and adequately to its proper place. This proper place, known to Dupin and to the psychoanalyst who intermittently takes his place, is the place of castration" [*PT*, p. 60; translation modified].

The psychoanalyst's act, then, is one of mere *recognition* of the expected, a recognition that Derrida finds explicitly stated as such by Lacan in the words he quotes from the seminar: "Just so does the purloined letter, like an immense female body, stretch out across the Minister's office when Dupin enters. But just so does he already *expect to find it* [emphasis mine-J. D.] and has only, with his eyes veiled by green lenses, to undress that huge body" [*PT*, pp. 61-62; original emphasis and brackets restored].

But if recognition is a form of blindness, a form of violence to the otherness of the object, it would seem that, by lying in wait between the brackets of the fireplace to catch the psychoanalyst at his own game, Derrida, too, is "recognizing" rather than reading. All the more so, since he must *correct* Lacan's text at another point in order to make it consistent with his critique. For when Lacan notes that the "question of deciding whether Dupin seizes the letter above the mantelpiece as Baudelaire translates, or beneath it, as in the original text, may be abandoned without harm to the inferences of those whose profession is grilling" [*SPL*, pp. 66-67], Derrida protests: "Without harm? On the contrary, the harm would be decisive, within the Seminar itself: *on* the mantelpiece, the letter could not have been . . . 'between the legs of the fireplace'" [*PT*, p. 69]. Derrida must thus rectify Lacan's text, eliminate its apparent contradiction, in order to criticize Lacan's enterprise as one of rectification and circular return. What Derrida is doing here, as he himself says, is recognizing a certain classical conception of psychoanalysis: "From the beginning," writes Derrida early in his study, "*we recognize* the classical landscape of applied psychoanalysis" [*PT*, p. 45; emphasis mine]. It would seem that the theoretical frame of reference that governs recognition is a constitutive element in the blindness of any interpretative insight. And it is precisely that frame of reference that allows the analyst to frame the author of the text he is reading for practices whose locus is simultaneously beyond the letter of the text and behind the vision of its reader. The reader is framed by his own frame, but he is not even in possession of his own guilt, since it is that guilt that prevents his vision from coinciding with itself. Just as the author of a criminal frame transfers guilt from himself to another by leaving signs that he hopes will be read as insufficiently erased traces or referents left by the other, the author of any critique is himself framed by his own frame of the other, no matter how guilty or innocent the other may be.

What is at stake here is thus the question of the relation between referentiality and interpretation. And here we find an interesting twist: while criticizing Lacan's notion of the phallus as being *too* referential, Derrida goes on to *use* referential logic against it. This comes up in connection with the letter's famous "materiality" that Derrida finds so odd. "It would be hard to exaggerate here the scope of this proposition on the indivisibility of the letter, or rather on its identity to itself inaccessible to dismemberment, . . . as well as on the so-called materiality of the signifier (the letter) intolerant to partition. But where does this idea come from? A torn-up letter may be purely and simply destroyed, it happens" [*PT*, pp. 86–87; translation modified]. The so-called materiality of the signifier, says Derrida, is nothing but an idealization.

But what if the signifier were precisely what puts the polarity "materiality/ideality" in question? Has it not become obvious that neither Lacan's description ("Tear a letter into little pieces, it remains the letter that it is") nor Derrida's description ("A torn-up letter may be purely and simply destroyed, it happens") can be read *literally*? Somehow, a rhetorical fold (*pli*) in the text is there to trip us up whichever way we turn. Especially since the expression "it happens" (*ça arrive*) uses the very word on which the controversy over the letter's *arrival* at its destination turns.

This study of the readings of "The Purloined Letter" has thus arrived at the point where the *word* "letter" no longer has any literality. But what is a letter that has no literality?

It seems that the letter can only be described as that which poses the question of its own rhetorical status. It moves *rhetorically* through the two long, minute studies in which it is presumed to be the literal object of analysis, *without* having any literality. Instead of simply being explained by those analyses, the rhetoric of the letter problematizes the very rhetorical mode of analytical discourse itself.

The letter in the story—and in its readings—acts as a signifier not because its contents are lacking, but because its rhetorical function is not dependent on the identity of those contents. What Lacan means by saying that the letter cannot be divided is thus not that the phallus must remain intact, but that the phallus, the letter, and the signifier *are not substances*. The letter cannot be divided because it only functions *as* a division. It is not something with "an *identity* to itself inaccessible to dismemberment" as Derrida interprets it; it is a *difference*. It is known only in its effects. The signifier is an articulation in a chain, not an identifiable unit. It cannot be known in itself because it is capable of "sustaining itself *only* in a displacement" [*SPL*, p. 59; emphasis mine]. It is localized, but only as the nongeneralizable locus of a differential relationship. Derrida, in fact, enacts this law of the signifier in the very act of opposing it:

> Perhaps only one letter need be changed, maybe even less than a letter in the expression: "missing from its place" ["manque à sa place"]. Perhaps we need only introduce a written "a", i.e. without accent, in order to bring out that if the lack *has* its place ["le manque a sa place"] in this atomistic topology of the signifier, that is, if it occupies therein a specific place of definite contours, the order would remain undisturbed. [*PT*, p. 45]

While thus criticizing the hypostasis of a lack—the letter as the *substance* of an absence—(which is not what Lacan is saying), Derrida is *illustrating* what Lacan *is* saying about both the materiality and the localizability of the signifier *as the mark of difference* by operating on the letter as a material locus of differentiation: by removing the little signifier "`" ," an accent mark that has no meaning in itself.[9]

The letter as a signifier is thus not a thing or the absence of a thing, nor a word or the absence of a word, nor an organ or the absence of an organ, but a *knot* in a structure where words, things, and organs can neither be definably separated nor compatibly combined. This is why the exact representational position of the letter in the Minister's apartment both matters and does not matter. It matters to the extent that sexual anatomical difference creates an irreducible dissymmetry to be accounted for in every human subject. But it does not matter to the extent that the letter is not hidden *in* geometrical space, where the police are looking for it, or in anatomical space, where a literal understanding of psychoanalysis might look for it. It is located "in" a *symbolic* structure, a structure that can only be perceived in its effects and whose effects are perceived as repetition. Dupin finds the letter "in" the symbolic order not because he knows where to look, but because he knows *what to repeat*. Dupin's "analysis" is the *repetition* of the scene that led to the necessity of analysis. It is not an interpretation or an insight, but an act. An act of untying the knot in the structure by means of the repetition of the act of tying it. The word "analyze," in fact, etymologically means "untie," a meaning on which Poe plays in his prefatory remarks on the nature of analysis as "that moral activity which disentangles" [*Poe*, p. 102]. The analyst does not intervene by giving meaning, but by effecting a *dénouement*.

But if the act of (psycho)analysis has no identity apart from its status as a repetition of the structure it seeks to analyze (to untie), then Derrida's remarks against psychoanalysis as being always already *mise en abyme* in the text it studies and as being only capable of finding *itself*, are not objections to psychoanalysis but in fact a profound insight into its very essence. Psychoanalysis is in fact itself the primal scene it is seeking: it is the *first* occurrence of what has been repeating itself in the patient without ever having occurred. Psychoanalysis is not itself the *interpretation* of repetition; it is the repetition of a *trauma of interpretation*—called "castration" or "parental coitus" or "the Oedipus complex" or even "sexuality." It is the traumatic deferred interpretation not *of* an event, but *as* an event that never took place as such. The "primal scene" is not a scene but an *interpretative infelicity* whose result was to situate the interpreter in an intolerable position. And psychoanalysis is the reconstruction of that interpretative infelicity not as *its* interpretation, but as its first and last act. Psychoanalysis has content only insofar as it repeats the dis-content of what never took place.

In a way, I have come back to the question of the letter's destination and of the meaning of the enigmatic "last words" of Lacan's seminar. "The sender," writes Lacan, "receives from the receiver his own message in reverse form. Thus it is that what the 'purloined letter', nay, the 'letter in sufferance' means is that a letter always arrives at its destination" [*SPL*, p. 72]. What the reversibility of the direction of the letter's movement between sender and receiver has now come to stand for is precisely the fact, underlined by Derrida as if it were an objection to Lacan, that *there is no position from which the letter's message can be read as an object*: "no neutralization is possible, no general point of view" [*PT*, p. 106]. This is also precisely the "discovery" of psychoanalysis—that the analyst is *involved* (through transference) in the very "object" of his analysis.

Everyone who has held the letter—or even beheld it—including the narrator, has ended up having the letter addressed to him as its destination. The reader is comprehended by the letter: there is no place from which he can stand back and observe *it*. Not that the letter's meaning is subjective rather than objective, but that the letter is precisely that which subverts the polarity subjective/objective, that which makes subjectivity into something whose position in a structure is situated by the passage through it of an object. The letter's destination is thus *wherever it is read*, the place it assigns to its reader as his own partiality. Its destination is not a place, decided a priori by the sender, because the receiver *is* the sender, and the receiver is whoever receives the letter, including nobody. When Derrida says that a letter *can* miss its destination and be disseminated, he reads "destination" as a place that preexists the letter's movement. But if, as Lacan shows, the letter's destination is not its literal addressee, nor even whoever possesses it, but whoever is possessed *by* it, then the very *disagreement* over the meaning of "reaching the destination" is an *illustration* of the nonobjective nature of that "destination." The rhetoric of Derrida's differentiation of his own point of view from Lacan's *enacts* that law:

> Thanks to castration, the phallus always stays in its place in the transcendental topology we spoke of earlier. It is indivisible and indestructible there, like the letter that takes its place. And that is why the *interested* presupposition, never proved, of the letter's materiality as indivisibility was indispensable to this restricted economy, this circulation of propriety.
>
> The difference I am *interested* in here is that, a formula to be read however one wishes, the lack has no place of its own in dissemination. [*PT*, p. 63; translation modified, emphasis mine]

The play of *interest* in this expression of difference is quite too interesting not to be deliberate. The opposition between the "phallus" and "dissemination" is not between two theoretical objects but between two interested positions. And if sender and receiver are merely the two poles of a reversible message, then Lacan's *substitution* of "destin" for "dessein" in the Crébillon quotation—a misquotation that Derrida finds revealing enough to end his analysis upon—*is* in fact the quotation's message. The sender (*dessein*) and the receiver (*destin*) of the violence that passes between Atreus and Thyestes are *equally* subject to the violence the letter *is*.

The *sentence* "a letter always arrives at its destination" can thus either be simply pleonastic or variously paradoxical: it can mean "the only message I can read is the one I send," "wherever the letter is, is its destination," "when a letter is read, it reads the reader," "the repressed always returns," "I exist only as a reader of the other," "the letter has no destination," and "we all die." It is not any one of these readings, but all of them and others in their very incompatibility, that repeat the letter in its way of reading the act of reading. Far from giving us the seminar's final truth, these last words, and Derrida's readings of them, can only *enact* the impossibility of any ultimate analytical metalanguage, the eternal oscillation between unequivocal undecidability and ambiguous certainty.

NOTES

An extended version of this essay can be found in *Yale French Studies*, no. 55-56 (1978) (special issue entitled "Literature and Psychoanalysis"), pp. 457-505.

1. In Edgar Allan Poe, *Great Tales and Poems of Edgar Allan Poe* (New York: Pocket Books, 1951), pp. 199-219, hereafter designated as *Poe*.

2. In Jacques Lacan, *Ecrits* (Paris: le Seuil, 1966). Quotations in English are taken, unless otherwise indicated, from the partial translation in *Yale French Studies*, no. 48 (1973) (special issue entitled "French Freud"), pp. 38-72, hereafter designated as *SPL*.

3. This article was published in French in *Poétique* 21 (1975): 96-147, and, somewhat reduced, in English in *Yale French Studies*, no. 52 (1975) (special issue entitled "Graphesis"), pp. 31-113. Unless otherwise indicated, references are to the English version, hereafter designated as *PT*.

4. "So infamous a scheme/If not worthy of Atreus, is worthy of Thyestes."

5. *La politique de l'autruiche* combines the policy of the ostrich (*autruche*), others (*autrui*), and Austria (*Autriche*).

6. Lacan, *Ecrits*, p. 57; translation and emphasis mine. Not translated in *SPL*.

7. Paul de Man, *Blindness and Insight* (New York: Oxford University Press, 1971), p. 140.

8. Stanley E. Fish, "How Ordinary is Ordinary Language?," *New Literary History* 5 (Autumn 1973): 52 (emphasis mine).

9. It is perhaps not by chance that the question arises here of whether or not to put the accent on the letter "a." The letter "a" is perhaps the purloined letter *par excellence* in the writings of all three authors: Lacan's "objet *a*," Derrida's "différance," and Edgar Poe's middle initial, A, taken from his foster father, John Allan.

The English Institute, 1977

The Program

Friday, September 2, through Monday, September 5, 1977

I. Biography
    Directed by Irene Tayler, Massachusetts Institute of Technology
    Fri. 1:45 P.M. How Wallace Stevens Saw Himself
                    Richard Ellmann, New College, Oxford
    Sat. 9:30 A.M. The Gypsy-Bachelor of Manchester: A Biography
                    of Elizabeth Gaskell's Creative Imagination
                    *Felicia Bonaparte, City College, City University
                    of New York*
    Sat. 11:00 A.M. Henry James and the Fiction of Autobiography
                    Millicent Bell, Boston University

II. The Achievement of Kenneth Burke
    Directed by Hayden White, Wesleyan University
    Fri. 3:15 P.M. Logology: Burke on Augustine
                    John Freccero, Yale University
    Sat. 1:45 P.M. Volume and Body in Burke's Criticism: or,
                    Stalled in the Right Place
                    Angus Fletcher, City University of New York
    Sat. 3:15 P.M. The Symbolic Inference, or Kenneth Burke and
                    Ideological Analysis
                    Fredric Jameson, Yale University
    Sat. 5:30 P.M. Colloquium with Kenneth Burke

III. Psychoanalysis and Literary Interpretation
    Directed by Geoffrey Hartman, Yale University
    Sun. 9:30 A.M. Critic: Define Thyself
                    *Murray Schwartz, State University of New York,
                    Buffalo*
    Sun. 11:00 A.M. The Notion of Blockage in the Literature of the
                    Sublime
                    Neil Hertz, Cornell University
    Mon. 9:30 P.M. The Frame of Reference: Poe, Lacan, and Derrida
                    Barbara Johnson, Yale University

Mon. 11:00 A.M. Instincts and Their Textual Vicissitudes
John P. Brenkman, University of Wisconsin, Madison

IV. Augustanism
Directed by Robert Elliott, University of California, San Diego

Sun. 1:45 P.M. Shaping The Augustan Myth: Literature and Its Contexts
Maximillian Novak, University of California, Los Angeles

Sun. 3:15 P.M. The Landscape of Allusion: Literary Themes in the Gardens of Classical Rome and Augustan England
John Pinto, Smith College

Mon. 1:45 P.M. Shaking Hands with the Universe with Graceful Negligence
John Traugott, University of California, Berkeley

Mon. 3:15 P.M. Some Nightmares of Augustanism: The Example of Swift
Claude Rawson, University of Warwick

Registrants, 1977

Gellert S. Alleman, Rutgers University; Marcia Allentuck, City University of New York; Paul Alpers, University of California, Berkeley; Quentin Anderson, Columbia University; Valborg Anderson, Brooklyn College; James Andreas, University of Tennessee; Jonathan Arac, Princeton University; Jacqueline Aronson; Richard Atnally, William Paterson College of New Jersey; Nina Auerbach, University of Pennsylvania;

George Bahlke, Kirkland College; C. L. Barber, University of California, Santa Cruz; James Barcus, Houghton College; Evelyn Barish, College of Staten Island (CUNY); Alan Barr, Indiana University Northwest; Leeds Barroll, National Endowment for the Humanities; J. Robert Barth, S.J., University of Missouri, Columbia; Beatrice Bartlett, Stephens College; W. John Bauer, Keane College of New Jersey; John E. Becker, Fairleigh Dickinson University; Millicent Bell, Boston University; Diana Benet, New York University; Carol Bere, New York University; Sara van den Berg, The Ohio State University; Carole Berger, Dartmouth College; Sr. Rose Bernard Donna, C.S.J., The College of Saint Rose; Warner Berthoff, Harvard University; Cecil Blake; Morton Bloomfield, Harvard University; Charles R. Blyth; John P. Boatman, United States Naval Academy; Felicia Bonaparte, City College of New York; Paul Bove, Columbia University; John D. Boyd, S.J., Fordham University; Frank Brady, City University of New York; Leo Braudy, The Johns Hopkins University; Peter Brazeau, St. Joseph College; David Breakstone, Massachusetts Institute of Technology; John Brenkman, University of Wisconsin, Madison; Leslie Brisman, Yale University; Marianne Brock, Mount Holyoke College; Leonora Leet Brodwin, St. John's University; Elizabeth Brophy, College of New Rochelle; Judith Gwyn Brown; Margaret M. Bryant, City University of New York; Lawrence Buell, Oberlin College; Daniel Burke, F.S.C., La Salle College; Kenneth Burke; Joseph A. Byrnes, New York University;

Margaret Canavan, College of New Rochelle; Cynthia Chase, Yale University; John A. Christie, Vassar College; Wendy Clein, University of Connecticut; James L. Clifford, Columbia University; Beverly Cogle, Vassar College; Wilfred Cole; Barbara Coley, State University of New York, Stony Brook; John S. Coley, University of Alabama, Birmingham; Lemuel B.

Coley, State University of New York, Stony Brook; Arthur Collins, State
University of New York, Albany; Margaret Comstock, New York Univer-
sity; Joel Conarroe, University of Pennsylvania; Philip Cooper, University
of Maryland, Baltimore County; Jean Dwyer Cormick, Rutgers College;
Eva Corredor, Douglass College; Sr. Francis Covella, College of Mt. St.
Vincent; Bainard Cowan, Louisiana State University; G. Armour Craig,
Amherst College; Jonathan Culler, Cornell University; Stuart Curran, Uni-
versity of Pennsylvania; William M. Curtin, University of Connecticut;

Winifred M. Davis, Columbia University; Roger Lee Deakins, New York
University; Robert DeMaria, Vassar College; Joanne Dempsey, Harvard
University; John DeWitt, Philadelphia College of Performing Arts; Morris
Dickstein, Queens College (CUNY); Evelyn C. Dodge, Framingham State
College; Charlotte Domke, Johnson State College; Stephen Donadio,
Middlebury College; Talbot Donaldson, Indiana University, Bloomington;
John H. Dorenkamp, Holy Cross College; Charles T. Dougherty, Univer-
sity of Missouri; James Downey, Carleton University; Anne Doyle, Mount
Holyoke College; Dan Ducker, Millersville State College; Georgia Dunbar,
Hofstra University; Thomas Dwyer, University of Toronto;

Delbert L. Earisman, Upsala College; Lee Andrew Elioseff, University of
Kentucky; Charles L. Elkins, Florida International University; Robert
Elliott, University of California, San Diego; Susan M. Elliott, University of
Hartford; Richard Ellmann, Oxford University; Martha Winburn England,
Queens College (CUNY); David V. Erdman, State University of New York,
Stony Brook; Sr. Marie Eugénie, I.H.M., Immaculate College;

Frances Ferguson, University of California, Berkeley; Anne Lathrop
Fessenden; Stanley Fish, The Johns Hopkins University; Angus Fletcher,
City University of New York; Ephim Fogel, Cornell University; Winifred
L. Frazer, University of Florida; John Freccero, Yale University; Warren
French, Indiana University, Indianapolis; Michael Fried, The Johns Hop-
kins University; Albert B. Friedman, Claremont Graduate School; Albert
Furtwangler, Mount Allison University; Virginia W. Furtwangler, Mount
Allison University;

Burdett Gardner, Monmouth College; Robert E. Garlitz, Plymouth State
College of the University of New Hampshire; Blanche H. Gelfant, Dartmouth College; Richard Gill, Pace University; Harry Girling, York University, Toronto; Arthur Golden, City College (CUNY); Barry Goldensohn,

Hampshire College; Lorrie Goldensohn, Goddard College; A. C. Goodson, Michigan State University; David J. Gordon, Hunter College (CUNY); Judith Skelton Grant, University of Toronto; James Gray, Dalhousie University; Robert A. Greene, University of Toronto; Dustin Griffin, New York University; Maxine Groffsky; Allen R. Grossman, Brandeis University;

Claire Hahn, Fordham University; Lynn Haims, New York University; Barbara Harman, Wellesley College; Maryhelen C. Harmon, University of South Florida; Richard Harrier, New York University; Phillip Harth, University of Wisconsin, Madison; Geoffrey Hartman, Yale University; Joan E. Hartman, College of Staten Island (CUNY); Richard Haven, University of Massachusetts; Grieg E. Henderson, University of Toronto; Suzette A. Henke, University of Virginia; Neil Hertz, Cornell University; Judith S. Herz, Concordia University; David W. Hill, University of Rochester; Rev. William B. Hill, S.J., University of Scranton; Margaret R. Higonnet, University of Connecticut; Elizabeth J. Hodge, New Jersey Institute of Technology; Daniel Hoffman, University of Pennsylvania; Laurence B. Holland, The Johns Hopkins University; Vivian C. Hopkins, State University of New York, Albany; Lillian Herlands Hornstein, New York University; Chaviva M. Hosek, Victoria College, University of Toronto; Dianne Hunter, Trinity College; J. Paul Hunter, Emory University; Daniel Hutchinson, Hatfield Polytechnic; Thomas Hyde, Yale University; Lawrence W. Hyman, Brooklyn College (CUNY); Virginia R. Hyman, Rutgers College;

John Iorio, University of South Florida;

Gabriele Bernhard Jackson, Temple University; Katherine R. Jackson, Bowdoin College; Nora Crow Jaffe, Smith College; F. R. Jameson, Yale University; Daniel Javitch, Columbia University; Judith L. Johnson, Columbia University; Michael Pusey Jones, University of Massachusetts, Boston; Sidney C. Jones, Carroll College;

Coppelia Kahn, Wesleyan University; Marjorie Kaufman, Mount Holyoke College; Carol Kay, Princeton University; Frederick M. Keener, Hofstra University; Veronica Kennedy, St. John's University; William H. J. Kennedy, Queensboro Community College (CUNY); A. B. Kernan, Princeton University; Karl Kiralis, California State College of Pennsylvania; Rudolph Kirk, Rutgers University; Judith S. Koffler, Rutgers School of Law (Camden); Theodora J. Koob, Shippensburg State College; Lawrence Kramer;

Richard Kuczkowski, New York Arts Journal; Maire Kurrik, Barnard College;

Craig La Driere, Harvard University; G. R. Lair, Delbarton; Robert Langbaum, University of Virginia; David J. Langston, Williams College; Richard J. Larschan, Southeastern Massachusetts University; Claudia Leacock, New York University; Lewis Leary, University of North Carolina, Chapel Hill; Nancy Leonard, Bard College; James Lehmann, Yale University; Lawrence Lipking, Princeton University; A. W. Litz, Princeton University; Marie-Rose Logau, Columbia University; Joseph P. Lovering, Canisius College; Sr. Alice Lubin, St. Elizabeth College;

Elizabeth MacAndrew, Cleveland State University; Warren J. MacIsaac, Catholic University; Paul Magnuson, New York University; Irving Malin, City College of New York; Leonard F. Manheim, University of Hartford; Ellen E. Martin, University of California, Los Angeles; Robert K. Martin, Concordia University; Howard A. Mayer, University of Connecticut; John Maynard, New York University; Richard McCoy, Columbia University; Thomas McFarland, Graduate Center (CUNY); Jerry McGuire; Terence J. McKenzie, United States Coast Guard Academy; Perry Meisel, New York University; Donald C. Mell, Jr., University of Delaware; Ronald Meyers, East Stroudsburg State College; Walter Benn Michaels, University of California, Berkeley; John H. Middendorf, Columbia University; Paul Miers, Rutgers University; J. Hillis Miller, Yale University; Alice Miskimin, Yale University; Raimonda Modiano, University of Washington; Geoffrey Moore, University of Hull; Robert D. Moynihan, State University of New York, Oneonta; James S. Mullican, Indiana State University;

Eugene Paul Nassar, Utica College of Syracuse University; Margaret R. Neussendorfer, University of Texas, Permian Basin; Richard C. Newton, Temple University; Donald R. Noble, University of Alabama; Marjorie Norris, Graduate Center (CUNY); Maximillian E. Novak, University of California, Los Angeles;

Agnes B. O'Donnell, Lebanon Valley College; Gerald O'Grady, State University of New York, Buffalo; Walter A. O'Grady, University of Toronto; Daniel O'Hara, Princeton University; Roger W. Oliver, New York University; James Olney, North Carolina Central University; Richard Onorato, Brandeis University; Stephen Orgel, The Johns Hopkins University; Charles

A. Owen, Jr., University of Connecticut; Patricia Owen, City University of New York;

Alex Page, University of Massachusetts; Stanley R. Palumbo, M.D.; S. M. Parrish, Cornell University; Coleman O. Parsons, Graduate School, City University of New York; Emily H. Patterson, San Diego State University; John P. Pattinson, New Jersey Institute of Technology; Felix L. Paul, West Virginia State College; Roy Harvey Pearce, University of California, San Diego; H. Daniel Peck, University of California, Santa Barbara; Alan D. Perlis, University of Alabama, Birmingham; Marjorie G. Perloff, University of Southern California; Carl A. Peterson, Oberlin College; Paul Pickrel, Smith College; Burton Pike, City University of New York; John Pinto, Smith College; N. S. Poburko, Dalhousie University; Ruth Prigozy, Hofstra University; Max Putzel, University of Connecticut;

Richard Quaintance, Douglass College, Rutgers University;

Fred V. Randel, University of California, San Diego; C. J. Rawson, University of Warwick; Donald H. Reiman, The Carl H. Pforzheimer Library; Emma S. Richards, Kutztown State College; Harriet Ritvo, American Academy of Arts and Sciences; Adrianne Roberts-Baytop, Douglass College, Rutgers University; Jeffrey C. Robinson, University of Colorado; Edward J. Rose, University of Alberta; Phyllis Rose, Wesleyan University; Shirley Rose, University of Alberta; Phyllis A. Roth, Skidmore College; Robert Roza, Swarthmore College; Rebecca D. Ruggles, Brooklyn College (CUNY);

Elaine Safer, University of Delaware; Edward W. Said, Columbia University; Paul Schiffer, University of California, Santa Cruz; Helen Maria Schmabel; Joseph Leandor Schneider, Curry College; Manuel Schonhorn, Southern Illinois University, Carbondale; Ronald Schuchard, Emory University; Harry Thomas Schultz; Paul Schwaber, Wesleyan University; Murray M. Schwartz, State University of New York, Buffalo; Arthur H. Scouten, University of Pennsylvania; Roger Seamon, University of British Columbia; Eve K. Sedgwick, Cornell University; Zulema R. Seligsohm, Hunter College (CUNY); Susan Field Senneff, Columbia University; Elinor Shaffer; Joan R. Sherman, Rutgers University; Heather Sievert, New York University; William Sievert, Pace University; Patricia L. Skarda, Smith College; Joseph T. Skerrett, Jr., University of Massachusetts; Sr. Mary

Francis Slattery; Janet L. Smarr, Harvard University; Alexander Smith, University of Connecticut; Robert Spiller, University of Pennsylvania; Rhoda McCord Staley, State University of New York, Stony Brook; Richard Stamelman, Wesleyan University; Susan Staves, Brandeis University; Holly Stevens; Roger J. Stilling, Appalachian State University; Donald D. Stone, Queens College (CUNY); Gary Lee Stonum, Case Western Reserve; Rudolf F. Storch, Tufts University; Michael Stugrin, Iowa State University; Maureen Sullivan, Marquette University; Donald R. Swanson, Wright State University; Peter Swiggart, Brandeis University;

Nomi Tamir-Ghez, Yeshiva University; Irene Tayler, Massachusetts Institute of Technology; Ruth Z. Temple, City University of New York, Graduate School; Elizabeth B. Tenenbaum, Herbert Lehman College (CUNY); Ralph R. Thornton, La Salle College; Patricia Tobin, Rutgers University; Jane P. Tomkins; Henry S. Traeger, Columbia University; John Traugott, University of California, Berkeley; Daniel F. Trompeter; Lewis A. Turlish, Bates College;

Steven Urkowitz;

Helen Vendler, Boston University;

Eugene M. Waith, Yale University; Melissa Walker, Mercer University in Atlanta; Emily Mitchell Wallace, Curtis Institute of Music; Patricia Wallace, Vassar College; Aileen Ward, New York University; Helen A. Weinberg, Cleveland Institute of Art; Philip Weinstein, Swarthmore College; Barry Weller, The Johns Hopkins University; Sr. Mary Anthony Wenig, Rosemont College; Hayden White, Wesleyan University; Epi Wiese, Harvard University; Joseph Wiesenfarth, University of Wisconsin, Madison; Marilyn L. Williamson, Wayne State University; Elkin C. Wilson, New York University; Calhoun Winton, University of Maryland; Joseph Wittreich, University of Maryland; Clara B. Woods; Samuel H. Woods, Jr., Oklahoma State University; Samuel K. Workman, N. J. Institute of Technology (Emer.);

Curt R. Zimansky, University of Colorado

Library of Congress Cataloging in Publication Data

English Institute.
  Psychoanalysis and the question of the text.

  (Selected papers from the English Institute; 1976–77:
new ser., no. 2)
    1. Psychoanalysis and literature. I. Hartman, Geoffrey H.
II. Series: English Institute. Selected papers from the English
Institute; new ser., no. 2.
BF175.E53   1978   809'933'1   78-7656
ISBN 0-8018-2128-2